MAKING GOD POSSIBLE

The task of ordained ministry present and future

Alan Billings

First published in Great Britain in 2010

Society for Promoting Christian Knowledge
36 Causton Street
London SW1P 4ST

The author and publisher have made every effort to ensure that the external website
and email addresses included in this book are correct and up to date at the time of
going to press. The author and publisher are not responsible for the content,
quality or continuing accessibility of the sites.

Unless otherwise noted, Scripture quotations are taken from the New Revised Standard
Version of the Bible, Anglicized Edition, copyright © 1989, 1995 by the Division
of Christian Education of the National Council of the Churches of Christ in
the USA. Used by permission. All rights reserved.
The extract marked 'RSV' is from the Revised Standard Version of the Bible,
copyright © 1946, 1952 and 1971 by the Division of Christian Education of the
National Council of the Churches of Christ in the USA. Used by permission.
All rights reserved. NB The RSV Apocrypha was copyright © 1957.
The extract marked 'AV' is from the Authorized Version of the Bible (The King
James Bible), the rights in which are vested in the Crown, and is reproduced
by permission of the Crown's Patentee, Cambridge University Press.

The publisher and author acknowledge with thanks permission to reproduce
extracts from the following:
Extracts from The Book of Common Prayer, the rights in which are vested in
the Crown, are reproduced by permission of the Crown's Patentee,
Cambridge University Press.
The extract from *The Alternative Service Book 1980* is copyright © The Archbishops'
Council and is reproduced by permission.
Graham Kendrick (b. 1950), 'From heaven You came', adm. by <worshiptogether.com>
songs excl. UK and Europe, adm. by <kingswaysongs.com>, <tym@kingsway.co.uk>.
Every effort has been made to acknowledge fully the sources of material reproduced in
this book. The publisher apologizes for any omissions that may remain and, if notified,
will ensure that full acknowledgements are made in a subsequent edition.

British Library Cataloguing-in-Publication Data
A catalogue record for this book is available from the British Library

ISBN 978–0–281–06228–7

1 3 5 7 9 10 8 6 4 2

Typeset by Graphicraft Ltd, Hong Kong
Printed in Great Britain by Ashford Colour Press

Produced on paper from sustainable forests

For Rudyard

Contents

Contents

Part 3
FUTURE POSSIBILITIES

Acknowledgements

I am grateful to a number of people for conversations had with them over many years around the various themes in this book.

There have been colleagues and students in the institutions and on the courses where I have taught: Ripon College, Cuddesdon, Oxford; Queens College and the West Midlands Ministerial Training Course, Birmingham; the College of the Resurrection, Mirfield; the Carlisle and Blackburn Diocesan Training Institute (now called the Lancashire and Cumbria Theological Partnership); the Centre for Practical Christianity, Kendal; the Urban Theology Unit, Sheffield; and the University of Lancaster.

I have learnt much from study days for ordinands and clergy: on the Yorkshire Ministry Course; in the dioceses of Swansea and Brecon, St Asaph, and Portsmouth; and from chaplains in the Royal Navy, Royal Air Force and Army, at Amport House, RAF Cranwell, RAF Cottesmore and Church House, Lubbecke. I was also introduced over several years to many different theological traditions represented by both clergy and laity at Theology Summer Schools in Oxford University.

But I have particularly benefited from having two evangelical curates, the Revd Jean Radley and the Revd Beverley Lock, who have taught me a great deal about their tradition, and in the process have become good friends. I hope I have done justice to what they showed me, but any faults are, of course, mine.

One of my greatest debts must be to the priest who first challenged me as a young man to think about ordination, Father Henry Evans, vicar of St Luke's, Stocking Farm, Leicester.

Finally, I thank Alison Barr of SPCK for her constant encouragement and support, and my wife, Veronica, who, as ever, has been patient during the writing.

Alan Billings
Sheffield

Introduction

Never let a crisis go to waste.
Rahm Emmanuel, White House Chief of Staff

This book is about ordained ministry in contemporary Britain – and its future. It takes the view that ministerial practice is shaped as much by changes in society and culture as it is by theology (though that is not always acknowledged by the Church).[1] The reason for this is that while the mission of the Church may remain the same from age to age and place to place, the institutional embodiment of that mission has to take account of particular and changing circumstances if it is to 'serve the present age' (Charles Wesley).

I could have written about the various ways in which ordained ministry is understood and practised within the different denominations and how each needs to change and adapt to meet the emerging future. However, because the Church of England has within it clergy who work with a range of different understandings of the Church, its nature and mission and, therefore, the role of the ordained ministry, I have chosen instead to write principally about the models of ministry found there. I believe they broadly reflect how ordained ministry is understood in most of the other churches, if not all.[2]

But to whatever denomination we belong, the most significant challenges facing the ordained ministry at the present time are common to clergy simply as clergy, and not because they are Methodist or Church of Scotland or Roman Catholic or Baptist or Anglican. It is with these common issues that I shall principally be concerned. As a result, I tend to use the terms 'minister', 'priest', 'clergyman' and 'pastor' fairly inter-changeably to mean 'ordained person' – except where one or other of these is more suggestive of a particular way of thinking about ordained ministry.

There is, however, one crucial respect in which the Church of England plays a role that is unique (though to some extent the Church of Scotland has a similar role in Scotland): it is the national Church. As a result I pay particular attention to the question of establishment.

The book's rationale

I have two reasons for writing. First, in a review of a previous book I wrote some years ago, Frank Field MP challenged me to think about the positive contribution that different traditions within the modern Church can bring so that they might work with and not against each other for the sake of furthering the kingdom.[3] I have tried to do that in relation to ordained ministry. Accordingly, I set out how and why those traditions developed and what seem to me to be their respective strengths and weaknesses today, before finally suggesting priorities for the future that draw from across the theological and ecclesiastical spectrum.

The second reason for writing arose out of the circumstances of my last appointment as an Anglican parish priest. During that time I was privileged to have two very talented women as curates who came from a theological tradition that was different from my own. As a consequence, I was forced to think about their tradition, how it envisaged the mission of the Church and the role of the ordained ministry, and how that compared and contrasted with my own understanding and experience. I had grown up as a member of an Anglo-Catholic congregation (they would now be called 'traditionalists'), and in my first years as a priest I was in liberal catholic churches (by which I mean those open to critical scholarship and new ideas in theology but tending to be more traditional in liturgical practice, following catholic styles of worship). My curates, however, were evangelicals. One was from a charismatic and fairly conservative congregation that had been unable to sponsor her for ordained ministry for theological reasons, would never have invited her back to preside and never did invite her back to preach. She came to us quite unprepared: she knew little of the Church's seasonal liturgies, their vocabulary and rituals; and while she encountered God in Scripture, it took some time before she understood how others found God in the sacrament. For her, the sacrament had no meaning outside the Communion service.

I imagine this situation is being replicated in many places now as the evangelical constituency grows and others shrink. As a result, there are more evangelical clergy than evangelical churches. Evangelical clergy accepting appointments in non-evangelical churches, therefore, have to think about how the mission and ministry of the Church is understood and practised there. So these reflections are offered in part as an attempt to chart some of the differences that exist in the contemporary Church and explain one to the other.

I want to look at the different ways in which Christians have thought about ordained ministry in recent years, the dominant models with which they have worked and that have inspired and motivated them, and why those models have taken the form they have. At the same time, I want to look at the sort of society and culture in which the ordained minister goes about his or her work today, since understanding that aright is crucial if ministry is to be effective. Finally, I want to look forward and think about the sort of ordained ministry the Church will need if it is to continue to contribute to the ongoing life of contemporary society. What is there in these different models of ministry from which we can all learn?

I will suggest that while key aspects of the idea of the ordained minister remain constant over time, the way they are worked out and their particular focus has to change as society changes – hence the importance of understanding the context rightly. As we look back over Christian history we are aware that much change has been organic and was relatively imperceptible at the time; changes in society and culture were less dramatic. But there have also been particular moments where the Church needed to respond more quickly, and when it failed to do so ordained ministry seemed to be in crisis – until the need for change and the type and direction of change were understood. Many would say we are passing through such a period of crisis at the present time. Perhaps this sense of crisis can be our starting point; we cannot afford to let this crisis go to waste.

The ongoing crisis

For as long as I can remember, ordained ministry has been facing a crisis – or so people have claimed. Since I was ordained in the late 1960s, books and articles have appeared at regular intervals on the subject of low clergy morale leading to stress or burnout or withdrawal from ministry altogether.[4] By the mid-1990s this was simply taken for granted. In the *Church Times* in February 1996, for example, the Dean of Salisbury wrote about a 'widely demoralized clergy' as if this were an incontrovertible fact. Similarly, in the same month, the editor of *New Directions* – a supplement with the Church of England newspaper – told us that 'clergy morale has reached an all-time low'.[5] As these two newspapers reflect the broad spread of Anglican opinion, we may assume that clerical angst was general at that time and not confined to one particular tradition of theology and ministerial practice. Since then, little has been written to suggest the position has changed in any significant respect. John Pritchard, the Bishop of Oxford (one of the Church of England's biggest dioceses), seems to think it may be worse. In 2007 he wrote:

> Many priests these days experience medically diagnosed stress at some time in their ministries. I'm no exception.[6]

3

The bishop does not tell us how many clergy this represents, but the number is large enough for him to regard it as a matter of concern. What might be of equal concern is the rather matter-of-fact way the bishop speaks about this, as if there were some inevitability about it. Even quite upbeat accounts of ordained ministry are written against a background of presumed underlying anxiety and bewilderment. They may be hopeful but they are not optimistic.

However, the causes of clergy stress have been diagnosed in many different ways: increased workloads, lack of support systems, inability to manage time, failure to take time out, the burden of buildings, being overwhelmed by occasional offices, a more secular age and so on. Whatever the diagnosis, it does seem to have affected numbers, which in turn affects workload and effectiveness: there has been a fall across all the mainstream denominations. If we consider the parish clergy of the Church of England, numbers have declined from just over 19,000 at the beginning of the twentieth century to just over 15,400 by the time I was ordained priest in 1969. By 1994 – when women were first ordained – the number was down to 10,449 and in 2006 it stood at 8,616 (of whom 1,507 were women).[7] Although the number of ordained women has risen steadily, their numbers have not compensated for the decline in male candidates, especially the drop in younger men. At the same time, the population has grown and parishes have been amalgamated. In other words, fewer clergy have been struggling to maintain more church buildings and minister to more parishioners, though with fewer worshippers; and this, it is said, has made them less effective.

But the decline in ordinations is symptom before it is cause. The truth is that in any occupation, people will feel depressed or stressed if they are unsure about what they are doing or feel that it is ineffective or not valued. Consider how the morale of the teaching profession sank during the 1990s as their role became confused and uncertain: just what did society expect of them? Were they about producing an educationally rounded individual, preparing their students for life in the most general sense, something that could not easily be tested and whose fruits would only show in adult life? Or should the focus be narrower, on raising academic standards that could be more easily targeted and tested? Then in the 2000s we had similar anxieties affecting social workers involved in child protection. Some were pilloried in the press because, it was said, they had failed to give parents support and had gone to the courts to have children removed precipitately;[8] but others, who had offered support, were condemned for not taking children into care more quickly.[9] The teaching and social work professions were left confused and demoralized.

It is because the role too of the ordained person in all denominations, though especially within the Church of England, has become increasingly problematic, both in society and in the Church, that clergy experience deep anxieties. This is not unusual; we have been here before in Christian history, though for different reasons. What is unusual is the seeming inability to adjust and articulate a convincing understanding of the role at this moment in time – convincing, that is, to both church members and to those outside. We need to work at what the new priorities for ordained ministry need to be for the contemporary situation, and that involves us first of all in taking stock of where we are and whence we have come.

There has also been an additional burden for the first generations of women clergy in that there have been no or few role models for them. One of my curates told me that when she was thinking about ordination she had only ever met male priests. The word 'priest' could only conjure up an image of someone male, much older and bearded! What was it, therefore, that she was being called to be and do? For those first women the temptation must have been to try to be 'like the men'. For the men the temptation must have been to judge the women by the pattern they had set. But the whole point of ordaining women was to bring something new to ordained ministry. The woman priest was not just the male priest without the beard.

But whether clergy are male or female and whatever particular gifts they bring to ministry as a result of their sex, or anything else about them, the question remains: What are they called to be and to do as clergy?

Making God possible

In his book, *The Pastoral Nature of the Ministry*, Frank Wright spoke about the time when, as a young curate, he was made to face the question: 'What am I for?'[10] At the regular Monday morning staff meeting he and his fellow clergy discussed the arrangements for the week: who would take this or that service, help with this or that pastoral situation. But what was it that made sense of these many and varied activities? What gave coherence to it all? In short: What are clergy for? If the question has not been asked and answered, ordained ministers find themselves responding indiscriminately to every demand: a ministry of ad hocery. There is no sense of priorities with the result that no task can ever be refused or given up – or rather, if we do refuse some request or fail to take up some initiative, we feel as if we have failed. We add; we cannot take away. The burden becomes intolerable. If, however, the clergy are afraid of facing the question of what they are for – because in their bones they are not convinced they will find a satisfactory answer – then the daily routine will feel more stressful, whatever we choose to do and however we choose to do it. In these circumstances no support systems however good, no management of time however efficient and no time-out however regular, can help.

I read Wright's book many years ago as a curate, but its haunting question has stayed with me ever since, compelling me from time to time to think afresh about what I thought I was doing and what I thought other people thought I was doing. What 'other people thought I was doing' is an important qualification. One of the drawbacks of much theological writing about priesthood is that it omits any reference to the perceptions of others – both believers and non-believers. Yet the question of what others think and the expectations they may or may not put on clergy is also a factor, I would say a very big factor, in ordained ministry being effective.[11]

Often we are not particularly reflective about the jobs we do. We think we know what it is to be a teacher or a journalist or a priest because, having seen other people at work, we have in the back of our mind a model. Models are what sociologists would call 'ideal types' – not 'ideal' in the sense of 'most desirable' but in the sense of being a coherent bundle of ideas that influence actual practice. As we look back over the twentieth century and the early years of the present century, we can find a number of models of ordained ministry influencing the actual practice of ministry. In Part 2 of this book I will look at some of these models, though we need to remember that it is never possible to find a precise model (the ideal type) exactly embodied in any particular person's ministry. Many clergy are deliberately or unconsciously eclectic in their approach, combining elements from different models. There has also been a proliferation of ways in which ordained ministry can be practised – stipendiary, non-stipendiary, ordained local ministry, chaplain, sector minister, team and group ministry, 'fresh expressions' – the list goes on. But speaking of models enables us to identify key features of actual practice.

As well as asking about the differences between the various models of ordained ministry we also need to consider what those different models have in common that enables us to speak of them all as examples of what it is to be an ordained person. I begin here because the sense of crisis is not related to any one model of ordained ministry but to the very idea of ordained ministry as such. It is the idea of the ordained person that is problematic in contemporary British society and that makes the exercise of the role more difficult in the first decades of the twenty-first century than at any other time in our history. This it is that creates the sense of crisis.

What are clergy for? Christians will want to give a theological answer to the question. But there is also a more sociological answer and it may be more illuminating to begin with that because so often the theological answer can seem far removed from day-to-day reality. Theological claims often seem inflated, and perhaps this mismatch between theological accounts and what is happening in day-to-day ministry contributes to the contemporary mood of anxiety. Of course, theology cannot just be set aside since what ordained ministers do in the end only makes sense in terms of their theological understanding of what they do. Nevertheless, what clergy do can be observed (together with what they say about it) and an account can be given. What do we observe? We can take a brief backward look in the most general way.

All through history and in almost every society some men (and sometimes women) have been singled out, or have stood out, because they seem to stand at the boundary between the world of mundane experience and the unseen realm of the sacred; or because they stand for the possibility of transcendent meaning.[12] At this level of generality we need not distinguish between prophets, priests, rabbis, imams, perhaps even shamans, or between those who have been chosen through some formal process (such as the recognition of a vocation, selection, training and ordination) or those who have commended themselves to others because of some charismatic gifts. These men and women bear witness to the reality of a sacred realm or transcendent meaning, and their role is acknowledged because the community itself accepts the possibility of such a reality or meaning, or at least is not closed to its possibility. It is accepted that this world – the world we know from sense experience – is not 'all there is' and its meaning is not exhausted by what science tells us. (We can already begin to see why the role of the ordained minister is problematic in Britain today.) For at least fifteen hundred years the people of these islands have become accustomed to looking for such people principally within organized religion and its ordained ministry.

As well as standing at the boundary between the everyday and the sacred and bearing witness, the ordained person has a further function: to make a 'relationship' with God possible. I put 'relationship' in inverted commas because this is not how every Christian would speak about what it is to have faith, and it would probably seem a strange way of speaking for much of Christian history. The idea of having a 'relationship with God' has come to the fore in recent years as a result of a shift in the culture more generally. We live now in a society that 'takes emotions very seriously' and regards emotional well-being – feeling secure and affirmed – as the key to happiness and the essence of the good life.[13]

In such a culture, human relationships are immensely important since they are the source of so many of our emotional highs (and lows). Television soaps bear witness to this as do the problem pages and lonely hearts columns of all national newspapers, both tabloid and broadsheet. If relationships with other human beings are so important for our well-being, a relationship with God – analogous in some way to human relationships – cannot be less so, hence the contemporary Church's preference for speaking about coming to faith as finding a 'relationship with God'.

But let us acknowledge the difficulty: whatever we mean by a relationship with God, it is clearly not the same as a relationship with another human being – someone whom we can see and touch and whose voice we hear – and to suggest otherwise is to give the honest seeker a misleading idea of what faith is. Moreover, if people are not very good at relationships, and those agony columns suggest many of us are not, we can sympathize with those for whom the idea of a relationship with God does not at first sound in the least bit inviting, simply an extension of the arena of trouble, neurosis and failure.

Perhaps there is a more helpful way of speaking about having faith than to speak in the first instance of a relationship with God. In a book about teaching Christian faith to young people, Helen Oppenheimer writes, 'The church is there to make God findable.'[14] I would change that slightly and say, the Church is there to make God possible. Since the ordained person serves the purposes of the Church, we may say that the fundamental task of ordained ministry is to help make God possible. What this means in practice will vary to a greater or lesser extent from time to time and place to place, depending on cultural circumstances. It may mean that simply by being present and visible in a community, the ordained person serves to remind people of God's reality. It may mean he or she helps people distanced from God by sin find ways back into God's presence. It may mean that in a time of anxiety or doubt or scepticism or disbelief, he or she has an intellectual task to make God credible. We shall need to explore these issues further, but to summarize, we can say that the ordained minister stands for the possibility of God and helps make God findable. This is the task that underlies the activities of all those who stand at the boundary of the seen and the unseen worlds, and who stand for transcendent meaning; the task, then, of ordained ministers.

But what happens when that boundary is not recognized, when a majority of people believes that this world is all there is, or that the only meaning life can have is the meaning we each give to our own individual lives? What happens to clergy in a society where people live without religion? It has been the slow realization that this might now be a true description of contemporary Britain that lies at the root of anxieties about ordained ministry. Does the idea of the ordained person still make sense in such a society? We need to examine, therefore, the accuracy of this perception of people's religious sensibilities – or lack of them – in Britain today. The answer to the question, 'What are clergy for?' in this part of the globe in the early decades of the twenty-first century very much turns on how we understand the contemporary culture. If we can get that right, the nature of the task facing ordained ministry will become clearer. Clergy will then continue to have a role to play, not only within but also beyond the observant Christian fellowship.

The book in outline

The book is divided into three parts. In Part 1 I will consider the context in which the ordained minister of today has to work – present realities – and how that context has refashioned the way the contemporary Church understands itself. If ministry is to be effective, we need to understand the context with all the insight and wisdom we can muster. In Chapter 1, therefore, I consider the important question of just how far Britain has become a secular society. In Chapter 2, I note the ways in which the Church over the past century has already made significant changes in how it understands its nature and mission, principally as a result of its responding to changes in society and culture.

This leads into Part 2 where, in four successive chapters, I look at the principal models of ordained ministry found in the Church today and seek to evaluate their relative effectiveness for the Church's mission. These are: the classical model of the parson; the evangelical model of the minister; the catholic model of the priest; and the most recent models of the social activist and the personal counsellor.

Finally, in Part 3, I will bring together a consideration of the likely direction of travel of British society for the foreseeable future and make suggestions for the way ordained ministry must reorder its priorities, drawing on the strengths of each of its working models and avoiding, where possible, their weaknesses. In this way ordained ministers will remain faithful to their vocation of making God possible for this generation.

But I begin with a consideration of the contemporary context in which ordained ministers practise.

Part 1

PRESENT REALITIES

1

Understanding the context

———•◆•———

We in this country, not uniquely, may be entering a world without religion, by which I mean a world without Christianity.

Kingsley Amis

We in England live in the chill religious vapours of northern Europe, where moribund religious establishments loom over populations that mostly do not enter churches for active worship even if they entertain inchoate beliefs.

David Martin

Clergy work out their vocation in particular contexts. If their ministry is to be effective, they need to understand, with as much knowledge and wisdom as they can find, what that context is like and, above all, its direction of travel. A key question for these times is, 'Just how secular is Britain?' This is not an easy question to answer. Secularization can be measured in different ways; the evidence is by no means unambiguous, and how it is to be evaluated is disputed. There is also a sense that we are still living through a process of cultural change that may not have reached its end-point. But clergy cannot wait on the outcome of the next piece of research. They have to minister on the basis of the best understanding they can bring to bear in their situation. How accurate is it to say, then, that Britain is moving inexorably towards a wholly secular society, a world without religion? What is the evidence? More particularly, how is the evidence to be understood?[1] What are the realities to which 'secularization' points?

A time of no religion

The term 'secularization' is used in two principal ways. In the first place, it has an institutional sense and refers to the removal from direct or indirect ecclesiastical control of such aspects of society as its law, its education and its government. In this institutional sense it can hardly be disputed that the Christian Church in the UK has lost, in a relatively short space of time, all of the power and most of the influence it once enjoyed. The Church of England had its origins in that period when membership of Church and state were synonymous. Initiation into the Christian religion through baptism was also initiation into civil society. The Church presided over key moments of family and community life – births, marriages and deaths – as well as great state events such as coronations and state funerals. Throughout the twentieth century that organic union of Church and state has gradually been coming apart, and the Church of England, together with all other religious groups, has simply become one voluntary association among many. It has a few residual privileges, but the presence of bishops in the House of Lords – the Lords Spiritual – and the local-government office of chaplain to the mayor are vestigial rather than expressions of contemporary realities. It is inconceivable now that a British Prime Minister would ever seriously seek the advice of an Archbishop of Canterbury on anything other than the most narrow range of issues (such as the remarriage of an heir to the throne), and perhaps not even then. The view of the Church on any matter is only listened to by government to the extent that it listens to the view of any interest group. Similarly, it is inconceivable that the Anglican Church, even with ecumenical partners, could ever again feel able to call the nation to a day of 'Fasting And Humiliation' as it did in 1853 (over cholera) or in 1854 (over the Crimean War) or in 1857 (over the Indian Mutiny). Church leaders would probably hesitate now before asking for a national day of prayer as they did in 1942 in the darkest days of the war. Throughout Europe, secularization in this sense is the norm in advanced liberal democracies where Protestantism has been the dominant form of Christianity. There is every sign that even those countries with a strongly Roman Catholic past (such as the Republic of Ireland) are going the same way. A test case for the power of the Church is whether it can still influence the state over those matters it feels strongly about, such as abortion law or stem-cell research. The evidence is that it cannot.

Once the Church was no longer able to influence the great institutions of the state, further secularization followed. The secularization of time is one example. Since the 1960s, Parliament has gradually relaxed the Sunday-trading laws. Contrast Sunday in today's shopping malls with the experience of a Swiss visitor to the Great Exhibition in 1851:

> Today is Sunday and I . . . walked down Cheapside which is quite a long street. I would have liked to have gone into a coffeehouse for a glass of ale or claret, but all the shops were hermetically sealed . . . On returning to my hotel I asked for my bill as I have been accustomed to settle my account every day. But the innkeeper politely asked me to wait until Monday.[2]

14

Even if we do not personally regret all the changes, they nevertheless mark a significant defeat for the biblical idea of a holy day in which the whole of society participated: 'Remember the sabbath day, and keep it holy.'[3] The association of religion and the rhythm of daily life – and this is only one example – is lost; and that is a very grave loss indeed because for many people, if not most, religion is about *performance* rather than belief.

In the second place, the meaning of secularization is extended to refer on the one hand to the way in which people in a particular society become less willing to affiliate to religious bodies or participate in religious activities, and on the other to the way people underpin their habitual ways of thinking with secular rather than religious assumptions. The first of these – religious affiliation and participation – can be measured (though not without difficulty); the second – habitual religious assumptions – is more difficult to be sure about. But this is a crucial area for Anglican clergy since (historically at least) they have seen themselves as having a ministry to those who, it is thought, may believe though without belonging.[4]

If secularization were to be measured solely in terms of churchgoing, then Britain (with the exception of Northern Ireland) is one of the most secular countries in Europe. A survey of English churches in 1989 found that little more than 10 per cent of people were present in churches on a given Sunday and less than one third attended occasionally.[5] Twenty years later and the churchgoing figure was below 7 per cent, with people attending less frequently. There are no signs that these trends are slowing significantly, let alone being reversed. For Anglicans, the fall in attendance probably began in the later years of the nineteenth century and continued relatively unchecked in the twentieth. There may have been a slight rise after the Second World War, but this was followed by a particularly steep decline at the end of the 1950s as the middle classes and women began to desert.[6] The Free Churches peaked in the late nineteenth century. For a while the Roman Catholic Church benefited from inward migration (largely Irish) and continued to grow until the 1970s.[7] Now it too faces the same downward trend in attendances at mass, despite the arrival of asylum seekers from Africa and migrant workers from Poland and elsewhere in Eastern Europe. The latter came as a result of the expansion of the European Union in the 1990s and the free movement of labour within its borders.[8]

Yet when the twentieth century began, Christians were in positive mood. The Archbishop of Canterbury, E. W. Benson, had declared in 1891 that it was 'well-known' that the number of churchgoers 'has largely increased and is still increasing',[9] and three years later C. W. Ainger felt confident enough to write in a hymn that 'the time is drawing near when the earth shall be filled with the glory of God as the waters cover the sea' – a reference to the universal triumph of the gospel. This was in some contrast to the deep gloom into which Christians had fallen when they digested the findings of the 1851 National Census for England and Wales. This had revealed that while most people might attend church or chapel occasionally, less than 40 per cent attended regularly.[10] By our standards these figures were impressive, but they deeply shocked and humiliated the Victorians, who thought Britain was a Christian nation. Horace Mann, the Anglican barrister who compiled and commented on the statistics, suggested a number of reasons for the low figures: untrained clergy, too few churches in urban areas, an insufficiency of free seats, a middle-class atmosphere and so on.[11] The churches responded robustly by opening theological colleges, building many new churches in the growing towns and cities and fiercely competing with one another for members. New churches were frequently built with far more seats than needed – the Victorians built with great expectations – and many were never filled to capacity.[12] But their efforts kept the proportion of church-goers just ahead of population growth until the last decades of the century and contributed towards Ainger's optimism.

The intense activity of these years also served to deflect attention away from the developing crisis of faith that was the real reason for subsequent decline. A growing number of people no longer believed in Christianity and many more were troubled with doubts. The poet Matthew Arnold saw this with an awesome clarity as early as 1867 when he wrote 'Dover beach' for the woman who had just become his wife. For him, the future held 'neither joy, nor love, nor light, nor certitude, nor peace, nor help for pain' because the Sea of Faith was ebbing away like the receding tide. While for some Victorians the disappearance of blessed hope was not loss but liberation, for Arnold the world he and his new wife would inhabit would be one where religious and moral certainty would give way to a terrifying confusion. Not everyone saw what was happening with the clarity of Arnold. One who did was John Henry Newman. As an old man at the end of the century he felt the encircling gloom of religious doubt. He believed that every civilization that was 'under the European mind' was 'tending towards atheism'.[13]

Late Victorian and Edwardian Christians had to wrestle with a range of challenges to traditional faith, especially biblical criticism and Darwinian evolution. While these intellectual issues at first disrupted the faith of the country's educated elite and only gradually affected the population more generally, the carnage of the First World War had an immediate impact on all social classes. How could Christian nations do this to one another? Where was God when men were dying in the trenches? Many turned their back on Christianity despite the best efforts of some of the chaplains (such as Geoffrey Studdert Kennedy, 'Woodbine Willie'), who had to rethink their theology fundamentally, especially the idea of God's impassability.[14] By the end of the Second World War the Church of England was beginning to recognize that there might be a problem. Archbishop William Temple commissioned a report (though he died before it was published in 1945), *Towards the Conversion of England*, which hinted at the underlying reality. It noted that to the casual observer Britain still looked like a Christian country: the monarch was crowned in Westminster Abbey, Parliament opened with prayer, religion was part of life in the armed forces and schools, the BBC had a Religious Department and so on. But 'behind the facade the situation presents a more ominous appearance'.[15]

For most of the twentieth century sociologists saw these cultural developments as confirmation of Auguste Comte's theory that secularization is an inevitable stage in the linear evolution of societies: as societies move from being organizationally primitive to being more complex and sophisticated, so they discard religious assumptions and adopt secular ones. This is especially true in the post-Enlightenment stage of human history as rational, scientific explanations for natural phenomena displace supernatural. It is often said, therefore, that secularization is a consequence of the scientific and technological revolutions that created the great urban centres of the industrial revolution. If the theory were correct, as the developing world industrializes and its population moves into cities, the secularization of culture will follow on a global scale.[16] However, more recently the secularization theory has been challenged, or at least qualified. There has been a realization that the United States, one of the world's leading industrial and urban nations, became more religious as people moved to the cities – perhaps for a while Britain did too – and has continued to register high levels of church attendance.[17] Similarly, the thesis does not seem to work in all European countries, such as Roman Catholic Poland. There is also ample evidence of religion flourishing among the newly urbanized populations of some developing countries.[18] Even in Britain some sociologists are revising earlier theories in the face of what seems to be a new interest on the part of some in spiritual matters.[19] This mild spiritual resurgence, however, has brought little comfort for traditional religion; far from it, for the new spirituality is marked by a repudiation of organized religion and its claims to authority in spiritual matters.

In saying that Britain is more secular than it was, we are also making a judgement about how religious the country used to be. This is also disputed territory. It is easy to assume a golden age, but perhaps what we thought was gold was merely gilt – and the gilt has been wearing off. But in saying that Britain is more secular we are not saying that it is wholly secular. What we need to understand is that the move away from what has been called an 'enchanted' world – a world in which little scientific knowledge was available and so causes were attributed to unseen spirits and supernatural forces – to a science-based knowledge, is not in itself evidence of secularization. People might come to understand volcanic eruption as the result of geological changes deep within the earth rather than the anger of God, but that might not lead to loss of belief, though it would lead to some adjustment as to how God and his relationship to the world is conceived. One form of religious belief did become unsustainable, but the death of one form of belief opened up the possibility of new forms. If we do not understand this process, we could only ever read the history of the world as the history of advancing and irresistible secularization.

What, then, are we to say about Britain? In my view it is more accurate to say four things – and this becomes a starting point for any discussion of future ordained ministry. First, religion has been 'democratized' so that when people are religious, they are not necessarily drawn into churches but do their own thing and are very eclectic. Second, most people are indifferent rather than hostile towards religion, which presents both a challenge and an opportunity. Third, as well as being more plural than it has ever been, Britain welcomes pluralism as good in itself.[20] And finally the 'cultured despisers' of religion have become more vocal and influential. Let me expand a little on each of these themes.

The democratization of religion

One feature of these times is what we might call the 'democratization' or 'computerization' of religion – as a visit to any large bookshop and its sections on religion soon reveals. Books of printed sermons – for which Victorian and Edwardian Christians had a huge appetite – are nowhere to be found. Shelves with Bibles and works of Christian theology can be found, but they are usually relegated to some obscure corner, a subdivision of 'World Religions'. They have been replaced by a far bigger and more prominent area reserved for a quite different kind of spiritual writing. In two of my local bookshops the relevant sections are labelled 'Mind, body and spirit' in the one and 'Spirituality' in the other. These shelves contain many volumes holding out the prospect of new forms of spirituality (a term preferred to 'religion', which suggests something organized or institutionalized) and spiritual experience.[21]

These new approaches reflect a general cultural shift towards a more emotional and expressivist culture and the attempt to find one's own spiritual path or one's own self. In so far as they all assume that human beings and the entire universe have a spiritual as well as a physical dimension, they are decidedly against a more secular, one-dimensional world; but in other respects they can be seen as the product of an age that has turned away from organized religion. They generally begin by attacking orthodox Christianity: the churches are not places to go if you want spiritual experiences, they are spiritually dead. They then offer various techniques designed to put you in touch with the spiritual side of your nature and with the Spirit that lies at the heart of the universe. The spiritual is reached not by looking outwards to God, as in traditional Christianity, but inwards to the self. What counts in the new spirituality is the quality of each individual's own spiritual experience. The individual becomes his or her own authority in spiritual matters, not the Church, not the Bible and certainly not the Church's ordained representatives. The emphasis is on positive experience, stressing the capacity of each individual to find his or her true self and enjoy spiritual blessing; it is never on what would be seen as the negative approach of some forms of Christianity with their insistence on the need for acknowledgement of sin and of repentance. Moreover, if one technique fails to satisfy, one simply moves to another – or combines several according to taste. Some of the elements of traditional religion can be employed – candles, incense, certain texts – as and when they are found to be useful.

This emphasis on the self and one's own experience as the ultimate test, combined with a pick-and-mix approach to the spiritualities on offer, are all marks of the consumer society. What has happened during this century is that a free market in spirituality has appeared. Spirituality is no longer the province of the churches alone. In addition, the focus on the self, and feeling 'good' about oneself, seems a far cry from Christian spirituality that speaks of denying oneself and losing oneself and taking up the cross. The emphasis on subjective feeling is a long way from a spirituality that points away from the self to the neighbour in need, urging people to go the extra mile for the sick, the hungry and the prisoner.

Religious indifference: a time of no religion

In the second place, we should note as a feature of these times the growth of religious indifference. In 2001–2, a research project by Lancaster University in Kendal, where I was a vicar, found that while only a tiny number of people described themselves as atheists, most people had no strong feelings about religion one way or another. Religion was not something they ever thought about and certainly not something they ever discussed; they were indifferent.[22] This seems to reflect the nation as a whole. It is not that people are convinced atheists or even agnostics; they simply have no interest in religion. For some, though not all, they have no 'feel' for it: it is as if they are religiously tone deaf.[23] This seems to have become the default position of the British – for the moment at least. We can call this a time of no religion.

We can trace the journey people have made to reach this point as we look back over the past one hundred years or so. In the first years of the last century, religion was a fact of daily experience, part of the texture of everyday life. In the home, there might be grace before meals, possibly even family prayers and Bible reading. Even when adults did not attend church, children would be sent to Sunday School. The Bible was taught as true in religious education lessons, and the school day would begin with a religious assembly – an act of worship – with hymns, prayers and readings from Scripture. That world has now gone. If we go back a little further to the late Victorian period, what characterizes the difference in the debate between believer and non-believer then and now is the decline in the cultural urgency of the question of religious truth.[24]

When and why did people become indifferent? One of the few people to recognize what was happening was the wartime chaplain we have already mentioned, Geoffrey Studdert Kennedy. He wrote a poem called 'Indifference', in which he related how at his first coming Jesus was put to death on Golgotha, whereas when he came to twentieth-century Birmingham, 'they simply passed him by'.[25] The poem was published in 1929, so we may assume that by then the more perceptive clergy had begun to notice a change.

Even so, while people may be indifferent most of the time, they are not indifferent all of the time. There are occasions when the ministry of the Church is still sought – baptisms, weddings, funerals and occasional services – and these should not be overlooked or their significance underestimated. We shall return to this theme and consider it in more detail in the final chapter.

The poet Philip Larkin had three tests for a novel: 'Do I believe it? Do I care? Will I go on caring?' In effect, people have asked the same questions of religion. They have not given a direct answer to the first question (they haver on the question of belief), but they have answered the second and third (they do not care about organized religion and they see no reason why their minds might change in future). Is this indifference a stage on the road from religious adherence to convinced atheism? Or is indifference rather than disbelief going to be the most accurate description of the settled attitude of most Britons in the early years of the twenty-first century? Can the situation be reversed? One sociologist of religion, Steve Bruce, has given a fairly unequivocal answer: a widespread, taken-for-granted but unexamined indifference towards religion has replaced a widespread, taken-for-granted but unexamined belief in Christianity; and this is unlikely to change.[26] However, we may be on safer ground if we say that we are in unknown territory. The final verdict will be crucial for ministry. My own prediction is that unless indifference is recognized and challenged — requiring a considerable intellectual effort at understanding why there is indifference and how it needs to be met (the subject of the final chapter) — it will eventually lead to unbelief. The residual knowledge and understanding of Christian faith that people have, that they draw on from time to time when confronted with issues of meaning or morality, will eventually not be renewed or refreshed and people will turn to alternatives. The most likely alternative will not be the militant atheism of society's elites – people find that as objectionable as militant religion – but forms of agnostic, secular humanism. This is more benign than aggressive atheism though probably more deadly in this time of no religion. It does not seek to root out religion as if it were something malignant, rather it co-exists with it, the way a family smiles on an eccentric, elderly relative, passing silent judgement.

The welcoming of pluralism

The third feature of modern Britain that impacts directly on religious faith is the fact that the country has become a plural society both in terms of religion and moral values. As far as religion is concerned, Britain is probably now one of the most diverse countries on earth. Every major faith is found in these islands. The oldest community, the Jews, have been here since the Middle Ages. They were often persecuted, and in the thirteenth century were expelled. Cromwell allowed them to return (he believed in religious toleration – except for Roman Catholics!). Their numbers have fallen considerably in recent years, now totalling about 300,000, though they exercise an influence on the life of the nation out of all proportion to their size. The other faiths have largely come with the post-war migrations.[27] They brought their faiths – Islam, Hinduism, Jainism, Zoroastrianism, Buddhism. The influence of these other religions has not been confined to their own faith communities. Indian religions, for example, have had a considerable influence on the development of the alternative spiritualities we noted above (sometimes called New Age), many of whose techniques and beliefs find their origins there rather than in Christianity. In recent years, Buddhism has had a particular appeal to those younger Britons who have been concerned with ecological issues and wanted to find a spiritual discipline that seemed to offer the possibility of serenity and calm in a stressful existence, but without too much dogma or clerical interference.

But it is not only religious faiths that have appeared in Britain. We have also seen the emergence of a secular humanism that offers a strong challenge to all faiths – as we shall discuss below.

21

However, it is not so much the fact of pluralism as its acceptance as something good that is now so striking. Until relatively recently the prevailing wisdom was that the nation could tolerate at the margin of its life a measure of pluralism in values, beliefs and ways of living, as long as one faith, Christianity, and its values ('bourgeois respectability', 'family values', 'the sanctity of life') remained dominant. This 'majority culture' would enable the nation to hold together, uniting around a common set of values and perspectives; but within this, minority cultures could be accommodated. Christians accepted this position pragmatically while making the private judgement that their faith was, of course, the truth, and looked forward to the day when the Christian monopoly would be restored. Government too, in so far as it thought about such matters, also assumed that while the country might be more multi-cultural than it was, there were underlying shared values that united the nation, largely, though not exclusively, derived from the Christian tradition. But as the immigrant groups became settled communities and began to assert themselves in the public domain, it soon became evident that there were significant differences between them. This came to a head when it became clear that Islam, a powerful presence as the largest of the minority faiths, challenged many of the assumptions of Western culture – the role of religion in politics, the place of women and men in society, attitudes towards gender and so on. The government scratched its head and wondered, therefore, what did unite the nation if it was no longer a common faith. Were there values that all British people shared, believers or not, that could be identified and promoted? The search for 'Britishness' began.

The debate about shared values soon petered out. Every attempt to say what they were met with resistance or, in some cases, derision. Finally, the government settled for the minimum any society needs to hold together: a measure of fairness and tolerance. But the debate has had an important effect. It became widely accepted that there were differences between us that were both fundamental and often irreconcilable. Many Christians began to take seriously the possibility that no one faith could have a monopoly of religious truth, neither should one religious community be privileged in any way.[28] Most people could only make sense of multi-cultural, multi-faith Britain by regarding all religious beliefs and moral values no longer as universal absolutes but as matters for private judgement. This is the major shift that has occurred – an acceptance of pluralism and a religious and moral relativism to which it has given birth.

There were other factors that contributed to this change of attitude. Modern philosophy has been dismissive of any claim to be able to comprehend the world and its destiny in some comprehensive theory or grand narrative – whether religious, as in the biblical story, or political, as with the Marxist view of history – or to hold moral positions that are universally binding. The suspicion of grand narratives and universal ethical systems came to be widely accepted at the end of a century in which vast numbers of people in Europe and across the world had suffered and died as a result of wars and conflicts with ideological roots. One group after another, each claiming to possess absolute truth, had sought to impose its views and its morality on others, leading to oppression at many different levels. At the level of the state, totalitarian regimes, sometimes embracing Christianity as in Fascist Spain, sometimes repudiating religion as in the Communist Soviet Union, had brought untold misery to millions of people. In the culture more generally, patriarchal ideas, deeply entrenched in traditional Christianity, had led, it was gradually and grudgingly conceded, to the oppression of many if not most women. By the start of the new millennium, therefore, many Europeans accepted the view that religion and morality were matters of private opinion and should not be imposed on others. This is a very significant change that has happened in a relatively short period of time, and it has considerable implications for evangelism and ministry. (How moral relativism squared with another firmly held conviction of the period – commitment to the Universal Declaration of Human Rights – is a paradox that remains unresolved!)

The cultured despisers of religion

I wrote above about the default position of the British towards religion being one of indifference rather than rejection. They were neither atheist nor agnostic but simply not interested. As a broad generalization that seems to be an accurate description, borne out by empirical evidence – and no less challenging to the mission of the Church. But while this was true of the majority, it was not true of all. In the final years of the last century and the early years of the present, considerable hostility has been expressed by some among society's elites. These people, occupying some of the commanding positions in the nation's public life, were becoming increasingly antagonistic and vocal. Well-known academics, broadcasters, journalists and cultural commentators began to write popular, polemical books and articles attacking religion, sometimes in quite strident terms. Two books that became best-sellers were *The God Delusion* (2006) by the Oxford professor Richard Dawkins, and *God is not Great* (2007) by the journalist and commentator Christopher Hitchens. The latter's book was subtitled in the United States, *How Religion Poisons Everything*, and in Britain, more mildly, *The Case against Religion*. (Hitchens seems not to have noticed that the atheist Communist regime of China made its attack on the people and culture of Tibet with the slogan,

'Religion is poison'.[29]) Then, in 2009, came advertisements on buses reading: 'There's probably no God. Now stop worrying and enjoy your life.' This campaign was prominently supported by Dawkins and the *Guardian* columnist Polly Toynbee, and received a great deal of media attention. Church leaders watched these developments with growing alarm. The head of the Roman Catholic Church in England and Wales, Cardinal Cormac Murphy O'Connor, said in 2008 that Britain was becoming an unfriendly place for religious people to live. But it was the perception that Lord Reith's BBC had fallen to the enemy that caused the greatest anxiety. Church leaders began to claim there was an anti-religious bias, a theme they repeatedly returned to. The Director General, Mark Thompson, a practising Roman Catholic, denied this, yet in January 2009 the Radio 2 broadcaster Jeremy Vine, a practising Anglican, argued in a magazine interview that both society in general and the BBC in particular had become intolerant towards the expression of religious views. 'You can't express views that were common currency 30 or 40 years ago', he remarked. He went on to say, 'Once I put my cards on the table about my faith in discussions, it becomes problematic.'[30] Much of this hostile commentary came after the attacks by Islamic terrorists on targets in American and European cities, and after revelations of abuse by Roman Catholic priests in several parts of the world – Australia, the United States, Britain and Ireland. But while these outrages gave the writers contemporary illustrations of the malign influence of religion in the world, the assaults on religion were not dependent on acts of religious terrorism or priestly abuse. Religion was found guilty of darkening minds and inspiring terrible deeds at every point in history and in every part of the world. It poisoned everything, and always had.

While these high-profile debates were taking place, there was also a growing alarm among Christians at what they saw as the influence of the cultured despisers at other levels of society. Headlines began to appear in newspapers that suggested that town-hall officers, National Health Service employers and state-school teachers felt under pressure to take measures that effectively undermined the position either of religion in general or Christianity in particular. We heard about civic Christmas celebrations that were turned into an innocuous 'Winterval' festival as town halls replaced their traditional 'Merry Christmas' banners with 'Season's Greetings'. Head teachers increasingly abandoned any pretence at offering a religious assembly, despite the clear requirement of the law, and stopped nativity plays in favour of seasonal, but secular, musicals. In 2009 a National Health Service nurse, who was an evangelical Christian, was reprimanded by her employers for praying with a patient (though after newspapers highlighted the case she was subsequently cleared of wrongdoing).[31] An opinion poll in 2009 found that a majority of Christians thought they were discriminated against in the workplace.[32]

Humanism is more than atheism and the denial of the transcendent. Modern, secular humanism is a developing philosophy and way of life that values the human and seeks, by appealing to a utilitarian ethic, to ensure the flourishing of all human beings of whatever gender or ethnicity. It is this secular creed that has been much more assertive in recent years. One can see its basic tenets informing, among other issues, the debates around euthanasia and physician-assisted suicide. At the moment this remains largely the faith of the social elites – the professional classes and intellectuals. But if it is not robustly challenged it will increasingly supplant Christianity as the faith of the British people as a whole – a theme to which I will return in the final chapter.

Yet a niggle remains. If the predictions of the early sociologists were proving correct and most people were growing indifferent towards religion, why were atheists so exercised with it? Books were written, newspaper articles penned and buses carried anti-religious advertisements. Perhaps this told us as much about the underlying insecurities of non-believers as it did about the health of organized religion. It may also reflect three other aspects of the contemporary scene to which the secularists are reacting.

First is the recognition that whatever is happening in the UK, globally religion is not in retreat at all but enjoying something of a renaissance.[33] This is not only true of Islam but of some types of Christianity as well, particularly evangelicalism and Pentecostalism. The inevitability of a non-religious future looks less likely if one takes a global as opposed to a merely north European perspective. In the UK too, while the absolute numbers attending churches may have fallen, this masks a more nuanced story of growth and decline, with evangelical congregations apparently flourishing.

Second, it is by no means clear at the moment in the UK that faiths other than Christianity are facing the same or similar decline. There is a little anecdotal evidence that the rising generation of Muslim young men is becoming less willing to attend the mosque. On the other hand, there are others who seem more determined than their parents' generation to profess their faith.

Then, in the third place, the gradual emasculation of religion in the public domain has also been halted in recent years. From the late 1990s, the British government began to take religion seriously and treat it sympathetically. This was partly because the Labour government and cabinet contained a significant number of believers. Tony Blair, Prime Minister between 1997 and 2008, was an observant Christian, Anglican while in office and Roman Catholic afterwards. His successor, Gordon

Brown, who remains Prime Minister at the time of writing, is also a Christian and a son of the manse.

But the interest in religion would have happened, irrespective of the beliefs of leading politicians, because of a growing concern about the cohesiveness of British society. Anxieties had arisen because with the passage of time, post-war immigration had changed the character of Britain's towns and cities as migrant workers became settled ethnic minority communities. Men who came here for jobs in factories and mills, transport and the National Health Service, sending their wages home to the West Indies or Pakistan, now had their families with them, often forming separate and extensive residential enclaves. Each subsequent generation was born here, and links with the original homeland became progressively weaker. Government worried that this would lead to social tensions at both national and local level. Their initial response was to see the different communities in ethnic terms, and the question of cohesion was addressed through anti-discrimination measures. Gradually, the importance of faith in defining identity was understood and the importance of the local places of worship recognized.

The government realized that religion could become a cause of division in urban areas, or a resource for fostering neighbourliness. The different religions, present in almost every urban area, had vital human and material resources. They had buildings, finance, people and long-term commitment. Most crucially they had the capability of nurturing in their congregations the attitudes and values necessary for building social capital and reaching out to others. While the interest in faith communities preceded the Islamic terrorist attacks in September 2001 in the United States and July 2005 in Britain, those events focused anxieties about cohesion and gave added impetus to the government's interest in faith communities.

Religion would not be parked and privatized but played a role in the public domain. It was, therefore, in the national interest to encourage faith groups to work in their respective communities, and through interfaith initiatives to build bridges between them. There were almost no other organizations that could do this at grassroots level. Faith, it was concluded, had a vital role to play in forwarding 'community cohesion'.[34] Despite the Dawkins–Hitchens thesis that all religion is bad, the government quickly learnt to distinguish moderate versions of Islam from the violent and extreme, and to cultivate and support moderate leaders. A Faiths Unit was created, initially in the Home Office, charged with the task of encouraging interfaith activities and interfaith networking. Religion was useful.

Even so, it was apparent that the country had moved a long way from the days when the position of Christianity in public life was assured and

taken for granted. Although Tony Blair said his faith was 'hugely important' to him, he knew that to mention it in public was unwise in the
British political context: even one's sanity might be called into question.[35]
His Director of Communications and Strategy, Alastair Campbell, refused to discuss the Prime Minister's faith with journalists, and famously
made it clear that politics was not a sub-division of religion: 'We don't
do God'. At the same time, the leader of the Liberal Democrats confessed
to being an atheist – something that would have been unthinkable in
the old Liberal Party, the repository of the Nonconformist conscience.
All this served to reinforce the view that it was becoming more difficult
to admit to being religious in a public context.

Summarizing all this, therefore, we could say that it would be as
big a mistake to characterize contemporary British culture as wholly
secular as to say that it is any longer wholly Christian or even religious.
What might be more accurate is to say that during the course of the
twentieth century, while the majority of people ceased to find religion
of any interest, there developed in Britain a free market in religion and
spirituality. There was no longer any compulsion – either legal or social –
for anyone to attend church. People were free to be religious or not
and to be religious in whatever way they chose, and most chose not to
be religious at all. Moreover, each individual became the authority in
religious matters, for only each individual knew what satisfied and
sustained him or her spiritually. Everyone felt free to asset-strip any of
the great religious traditions and take from them whatever they pleased
or whatever seemed to help. In such a culture, the last remaining privileges of the Church simply looked out of place – either harmlessly so
or offensively so – and slowly had to give way. The chief loser among
the Christian churches was the Church of England, so that its ordained
ministry has been most troubled by this whole period and process.

The challenge of the modern state

As well as these cultural changes, the twentieth century also saw the full
flourishing of the modern, democratic state. This too had considerable
implications for the Church and its ministry. Let me highlight three
aspects of this that again have a direct bearing on ordained ministry.

An educated democracy

The modern state has its origins, of course, in an earlier period. The
roots of the Parliamentary system lie in the seventeenth century, with
the struggle between king and Parliament, while the American and
French revolutions of the following century set in train the idea of the
fully democratic state. But we forget that universal suffrage was only

finally realized in the 1920s when women were able to vote. By then the nation had come to recognize that if it were to be both democratic and prosperous it would need an educated people. Between 1870 and 1944 a series of landmark Education Acts was passed that eventually resulted in a system of compulsory but free education to secondary age for the whole population. By the early years of the new millennium, between 35 and 40 per cent of the population was receiving higher education of some kind. From the mid-twentieth century, therefore, we have had a more educated and prosperous people, schooled in democracy. This had profound consequences for the Protestant churches, especially the Church of England. It led in the first place to lay people seeking a more democratic Church. Democratic habits and instincts, once learnt, were not going to be confined to the political sphere alone. Lay people wanted to play a more responsible role in the management of the Church. The development of synodical government in the Church of England was a direct, though incomplete, response to these pressures. In the second place, an educated laity presented the clergy with a considerable challenge. For most of Anglican history, the parish priest was at least as well educated and probably better educated than anyone else in either congregation or parish. This became less true during the course of the twentieth century. But competent and educated lay people did not leave their enquiring minds on hold when it came to matters of theology and its relevance to modern issues. They expected robust debate in the Church and a certain standard of preaching and teaching, especially in a Church that historically had set some store by a learned and intelligent exposition of the Christian message in the light of modern knowledge. When they were disappointed they turned to secular cultural commentators. In many ways, the columnists on national newspapers have become the popular preachers of our times – some thoughtful, some evangelical and some positively ranting.

The welfare state and its pastors

The modern, democratic state is also a welfare state. The creation of the welfare state led to the rapid growth of new, caring professions. When George Herbert wrote his manual for priests in the seventeenth century, he took it for granted that the clergyman had a major role to play in the life of the local community.[36] He also assumed that his role would be multi-faceted and extend far beyond his religious duties: he would have to be a schoolmaster, a dispenser of charity, a law enforcement officer, even a doctor and pharmacist. In many parts of the country the parson would be the only person performing these tasks. He had to be knowledgeable, therefore, across a range of subjects, and this suggested that priests should be educated and resident. In many respects this situation continued until the nineteenth century, when some occupations – teaching, law and medicine – professionalized and effectively robbed the clergyman of these roles.[37] This left the more directly pastoral aspects of parish work. But with the founding of the modern welfare state by the post-Second World War Labour government the pastoral tasks remaining to the clergy were slowly eroded as well. The working classes became better educated and more able to take control of their lives. New professional groups gradually emerged and took over almost every other pastoral function of the clergy. Priests ceased to be the sole pastors in their parishes. They also ceased to be the most effective pastors in their parishes. Pastoral care was now offered by a range of people: social workers, health visitors, community nurses, therapists, counsellors. As the years passed the numbers and the specialisms grew. Amid so many trained and qualified people the clergy came to look like amateurs in pastoral care, not least to themselves. This came as a hammer blow since it undermined their one claim to social usefulness – the offer of pastoral care – that had survived the climate of growing secularization and the loss of spiritual authority.

The flight from traditional community

At the same time as Britain became a more secular society, it also became a less traditional one. Indeed, this process has contributed to secularization. In traditional societies, the acceptance of a common religion is one of the factors that makes for group identity and cohesion. In such societies belief and value systems, norms and patterns of behaviour are simply passed on and adopted by each successive generation. In a post-traditional society this 'taken-for-grantedness' of beliefs is undermined by pluralism.[38] People *choose* the beliefs, the morality and the values by which they live. Greater prosperity allowed Britons to opt for greater choice; a proliferation of lifestyles, beliefs and values followed. One consequence of this was the undermining of communities – inner-city, suburban, rural – since communities are the result not simply of people living in close geographical proximity but also of having shared beliefs and values.

The collapse of the traditional community was aided by other factors as well. In towns, the dispersal of tight-knit working-class populations to peripheral estates snapped the bonds of community and enabled people to opt for more private lives. This wish for a more private way of life undermined the sense of community in suburbia as well. For communities to be created there must be regular contact between people over a period of years, with some sense of shared values. Communities are created when people meet informally in local shops and streets, and socially in pubs, clubs and churches on a regular basis. But with greater mobility, people were able to live in one place, work in another, shop in a third and spend their weekends elsewhere altogether.

Similar patterns affected the countryside. The car made possible a new kind of resident in rural areas – commuters – for whom the village was home but not necessarily the place where they worked, shopped, based their social life or sent their children to school. Rural pubs, schools, post offices, shops and even bus services were all adversely affected (and rural railways had already gone by the time I started my ministry in the late 1960s, thanks to the closing of many lines following Dr Richard Beeching's 1955 Modernization Plan – the 'Beeching Axe').

There was gain as well as loss in all this. The loss was the sense of being part of a (geographical) community. The gain was freedom – for communities impose norms of behaviour and attitude that can be restrictive and intrusive. The post-1960s generations wanted freedom to live, think and behave, not according to some predetermined norms but according to each person's own desires. They wanted freedom to opt in and out of a new style of 'community' – the associations, clubs and interest groups to which they belonged voluntarily. It seemed that freedom and community could not co-exist. Anglican parish clergy invested heavily in the idea of geographical community. They backed the wrong horse.

Conclusion

An historian writing about Britain in the nineteenth century is compelled to speak about Christianity and its role in the life of the nation at every level. In contrast, historians of the twentieth century felt no such compulsion; religion might not even be mentioned, except as a footnote or with reference to the religion of post-war immigrant groups. Throughout the twentieth century, Britain became more secular – not in the sense that people became convinced atheists, though increasing numbers did, but rather in that they became indifferent to religion: some ceased to have any feel for it; some became less convinced that it could contribute much to how they lived; many found their understanding of God and his relationship to the world less clear. As a consequence, religion ceased to be part of the texture of their lives. The core of this phenomenon and what we principally mean by secularization is, therefore, as Steve Bruce has written, 'that the lives of fewer people . . . are influenced by religious beliefs' of any kind.[39] This is contemporary Britain: it is a time of no religion.

Even though the instinct for religion has not been totally snuffed out, there is little prospect of any dramatic reversal of this situation of religious indifference because Christianity is no longer being communicated to each succeeding generation at the crucial points of transmission – in the home, at Sunday School and in morning assembly. For the Church as an institution this has resulted in the gradual erosion of its once dominant and privileged place in society. What remains often seems anachronistic and sometimes offensive. In addition, substantial and continuing inward migration has resulted in Christianity becoming once again one faith among many in a religious market place, competing for adherents, though now with fewer potential customers – a new situation in the early decades of the third millennium. But a rival faith has also appeared in the form of an aggressively evangelistic, secular humanism. For the ordained ministry it has led to a challenge to both religious and pastoral functions, undermining the clergy's sense of social usefulness and hence their confidence.

These cultural and societal changes led the Church to rethink how it understood itself, both its nature and its purpose. This is the subject of the next chapter.

2

How the Church thinks about itself

All churches either rise or fall as the Ministry doth rise or fall – not in riches or worldly grandeur – but in knowledge, zeal and ability for their work.

Richard Baxter

The Christian Church does not exist in a vacuum. Throughout its long history it has been affected by changes in society and culture that often lay beyond its capacity to influence. This has certainly been more the case in recent centuries as the Age of Christendom – when the Church could profoundly influence culture and society – has come to an end. But the Church has also changed as a result of its own reflection. The two are not unconnected: it was often a shift in the culture more generally that led the Church, or forced the Church, to reflect further on its own life and mission. In five areas in particular the Church in the twentieth century began to reappraise the way it understood both its nature and its task. We take these changes somewhat for granted now, forgetting how recent the developments have been. I will look briefly at each in turn, and then reflect on the way these changes in the Church's understanding of itself, its life and mission, impacted on the role of the ordained ministry.

Changes in the Church's self-understanding

Church as denomination

At some point during the course of the twentieth century each of the mainline Protestant churches, including the Church of England, came to think of itself as one Christian denomination among many rather than as the most authentic expression of Christianity in the UK, if not the world (the Roman Catholic Church at best havered). There was an acknowledgement on the part of each that they might not possess the whole truth and that there might be things to learn from other Christian churches. This represented a profound shift in thinking. At the end of the previous century there had been considerable competition between all the Christian churches, based on quite opposite assumptions.

These assumptions were most clearly articulated by the Roman Catholic Church. It taught, for example, that 'the one and true Church is the community of men brought together by the profession of the same Christian faith and conjoined in the communion of the same sacraments, under the government of the legitimate pastors and especially the one vicar of Christ on earth, the Roman pontiff.'[1] Although these words were spoken in the sixteenth century, they have been reiterated by the Roman Catholic Church in one form or another in every century since. The high-water mark of this thinking was reached at the end of the nineteenth century, with the declaration in 1870 of Papal Infallibility. It was in the light of that teaching that English Roman Catholic congregations have been singing the hymn 'Faith of our fathers' ever since. The hymn speaks of the need for the conversion to the true faith, not of non-believers but of other Christians, through the intercessions of Mary:

> Faith of our fathers, Mary's prayers,
> shall win our country back to thee;
> and through the truth that comes from God
> England shall then indeed be free.[2]

In other words, the Roman Catholic Church, and it alone, was and is the Christian Church.

In the nineteenth century, the adherents of all the churches tended to see their own church in similar terms (though some evangelicals thought the true church was invisible and consisted of themselves and other true believers who were known only to God and might be found in any church). This understanding of the Church provided Christians with urgent missional incentives and a clear evangelistic goal since they alone could preach the authentic Christian message that people needed to hear if they were to be saved. (This attitude continued well into the twentieth century among some Christians. I have a boyhood memory of some members of a free Evangelical church coming to the Anglo-Catholic church where I was a choirboy and chaining themselves to the chairs as they made their protests against what they believed was an erroneous form of Christianity. At the elevation of the host they cried out that this was a blasphemy. For the rest of the service several men struggled to lift them up still chained in their chairs and carry them outside, where they continued to harangue the congregation as they left. I was particularly struck by a banner that said that people like me were 'destined for perdition'.) The history of Christianity in the mission fields in the nineteenth century is the history of these denominational rivalries working themselves out. Yet it was among the missionaries that the first suggestion of a change came. In 1910 the Edinburgh Conference brought together missionaries from most of the churches and the denominational missionary societies, to consider together how they might evangelize more effectively and less competitively. It was a time of great optimism combined with great urgency, as the slogan of the conference – 'the evangelization of the world in this generation' – makes clear. Neither the Eastern Orthodox Churches nor the Roman Catholic Church – the majority of Christians – was invited. But the conference laid the foundations for the eventual formation in 1948 of the World Council of Churches.

By the middle of the twentieth century, the Protestant churches were learning to see themselves as part of the Christian Church and not the whole of it, or as an expression of the universal Church that lay beyond each of them. They thought of themselves, in other words, as 'denominations' rather than the Church. They even gave this a name: ecumenicalism or ecumenism. Although ecumenism began as a movement to bring about a united Christian Church – 'the coming great Church' – almost all the attempts at uniting in the UK, such as those of the Church of England and the Methodist Church, came to nothing. One exception was the amalgamation of the Presbyterian Church of England and the Congregational Church in England and Wales in 1972 to form the United Reformed Church.[3] Ecumenism is now rarely more than an acceptance of denominationalism.

But denominationalism (ecumenism) proved problematical for Anglican clergy. The Church of England had been constituted by Act of Parliament and organized as if it were the Church of and for all the English people and not a denomination: it was the established Church. This was why it was a broad Church: it sought to embrace as far as possible the range of Christian views. Everyone in the country, simply by being resident, was conscripted into an Anglican parish. Richard Hooker gave classic expression to the Anglican ideal when he wrote that there was not a member of the commonwealth who was not a member of the Church of England and not a member of the Church of England who was not a member of the commonwealth.[4] But this Anglican ideal, never easy to justify (and rendering evangelism unnecessary since everyone was Anglican by birth), became increasingly questionable after 1851, when the religious Census revealed that there were almost as many Nonconformists in the country as there were Anglicans.[5] During the course of the twentieth century the justification for Anglican hegemony drained away completely with the steady rise in the number of non-believers, the decline of Anglican membership and the growth of the Roman Catholic constituency – the result of inward migration from Ireland, the Commonwealth and Eastern Europe. Many Anglican clergy found this deeply unsettling. If most people were (possibly) not Christians and most Christians were not Anglicans, how could Church of England clergy continue to behave as if the exact opposite were true? Denominationalism/ecumenism leads inexorably to unease with establishment. The discomfort was not made any easier by the appearance in the post-Second World War period of growing numbers of people of other faiths. Although there have been adherents of other faiths in the country for many centuries, it was the visible presence of sacred buildings – mosques, temples and gurdwaras – in most English towns and cities that made these minorities impossible to ignore.

But what caused this change in thinking and led to denominationalism and ecumenism? It is probably best understood as one consequence of a more general shift in the culture – the so-called 'expressive revolution'. The culture of the later twentieth century, the result of a prolonged period of relative prosperity, universal education and freedom, was marked by what has been called a 'turn to the self' – a focus on the self and its wholeness. This had a profound effect on how people thought about religion and about themselves as spiritual beings. Religion was understood not so much as something pre-packaged to be received but as a quest to be embarked upon. It was not about being conformed to something predetermined but about seeking and searching for oneself. Attitudes towards the different churches changed in the light of this. People came to think of them not as mutually exclusive guardians of Christian truth where only one could be right and all others must be mistaken, but as repositories of different religious resources that might not necessarily be incompatible. In the quest for an authentic faith one might find help in any of the churches. This had the effect of relativizing all traditions.

Denominationalism was, then, a reflection of the relativization of all Christian churches and the feeling that those things that had divided Christians in the past – matters of belief, liturgy and church order – were no longer of such significance. Salvation was no longer thought of as confined to the members of any one of the churches, perhaps not even to the Church. The churches ceased to be competitive in the way they had been in the nineteenth century, and growing numbers of people sought spiritual resources wherever they thought they could be found. While greater co-operation and friendliness between Christians of different denominations was to be welcomed, it did tend to blunt the commitment to evangelism – so much so that by the end of the century a decade of evangelism had to be proclaimed to remind churches of the need to make converts!

But denominationalism has had a further unforeseen consequence that is of the greatest significance: it has made it relatively easy for Christians to move from one denomination to another. At the beginning of the twentieth century churches were highly competitive and highly suspicious of one another. To move from one to another was a very significant act. Today, people will move with relative ease between denominations. In marketing terms, we could say there is less brand loyalty than there used to be. Increasingly, people attend a particular church because it meets their religious needs or happens to be the nearest, and not because of any denominational allegiance.[6]

I suggested above that the Roman Catholic Church had never quite embraced ecumenism with the enthusiasm of other denominations. It entered into conversations on points of doctrine, yet continued to insist that 'full unity' would only come about 'when all share in the fullness of the means of salvation entrusted by Christ to his Church' – which is another way of saying that all Christians must submit to Rome.[7] As a result, mixed signals came from it throughout the century. On the one hand, it has shown an increasing willingness to be part of the ecumenical movement at every level, while on the other it has from time to time done something that has caused fellow Christians to wonder. The publication in 1998 of a teaching document on the Eucharist, *One Bread One Body*, was one example.[8] For many years some Roman Catholic parish priests had been giving the sacrament to non-Roman Catholics in certain circumstances and, they believed, with their bishop's tacit support – for example, to the non-Roman Catholic partner of a mixed marriage or in small ecumenical gatherings. These practices were abruptly stopped as a result of this document, leaving many people hurt and puzzled.

In case there was any doubt about the position of the Roman Catholic Church, the Congregation for the Doctrine of the Faith published a document in 2007 reaffirming the traditional teaching that Protestant churches were not churches in the fullest sense. It posed a series of questions and answers on 'certain aspects of the doctrine on the Church' that included the following:

Second Question
What is the meaning of the affirmation that the Church of Christ subsists in the Catholic Church?

Response
Christ 'established here on earth' only one Church and instituted it as a 'visible and spiritual community', that from its beginning and throughout the centuries has always existed and will always exist, and in which alone are found all the elements that Christ himself instituted . . . This Church, constituted and organized in this world as a society, subsists in the Catholic Church, governed by the successor of Peter and the Bishops in communion with him.
. . .

Fifth Question

Why do the texts of the [Second Vatican] Council and those of the Magisterium since the council not use the title of 'Church' with regard to those Christian Communities born out of the Reformation of the sixteenth century?

Response

According to Catholic doctrine, these communities do not enjoy apostolic succession in the sacrament of Orders, and are, therefore, deprived of a constitutive element of the Church. These ecclesial Communities which, specifically because of the absence of the sacramental priesthood, have not preserved the genuine and integral substance of the Eucharistic Mystery cannot, according to Catholic doctrine, be called 'Churches' in the proper sense.

There is little sign that the Roman Catholic Church is prepared to move from this position in its formal teaching, especially under the conservative Pope Benedict XVI, who was Prefect of the Congregation for the Doctrine of the Faith before his election as Pope. But at local level, relationships between the Roman Catholic Church and other churches are often very fruitful, not least in a willingness to work with fellow Christians on justice and peace issues and to participate fully in the Week of Prayer for Christian Unity.

Church as pilgrim people

A second significant shift in the way Christians thought of the Church during the twentieth century was a movement away from thinking of it primarily as an institution to thinking of it in more dynamic terms as the pilgrim people of God. This also enabled Christians to think of the Church in more democratic and less hierarchical ways. George Lindbeck summed up the essence of this view in this way:

> The church is a band of men and women traveling towards the promised land: God's kingdom of justice, righteousness, peace and love. As they travel towards this goal they are stained with the dust of the journey, frequently weary, bedraggled and complaining, inclined to forget their destination and tempted to turn aside and settle down, yet repeatedly impelled by their memories and hopes to press forward.[9]

The image of the pilgrim people, lay and ordained, journeying together was in some contrast to certain previous ecclesiologies. The Roman Catholic scholar, Henri de Lubac, for example, writing in 1956, spoke about 'two categories' of persons within the Church, one active and one passive, 'pastors and flock, Church teaching and Church taught, Church ruling and governed, clergy and laity, hierarchy and faithful, ministers and subjects of sacraments – or, as was once said, sacerdotes and idiotes'.[10] The image of the pilgrim people of God caught the imagination and mood of all the churches. The Roman Catholic Church used it, though not consistently, in its documents on the Church at the Second Vatican Council.

There were several reasons for the emergence of this particular metaphor at that moment in time. There was first a general and growing disillusionment with all institutions, not simply the Church. The image of people on a journey suggested a dynamic movement, open to change and new possibilities, rather than a static organization. Second, the growing democratic spirit made people uneasy about unaccountable and hierarchical bodies – again, this was a general feeling about all organizations and not just the Church. It is a feeling that has not diminished over the years. If anything, people have become more frustrated. There was also an increasing desire on the part of a more educated and articulate laity to play a greater role in the affairs of the Church.[11] Finally, we have already noted that the spirituality of the times was influenced by an expressive culture that placed an emphasis on searching rather than passively accepting – exploring and journeying towards the truth, seeking one's own spiritual path. In addition, modern scholarship gave theological and biblical underpinning to these changes. According to the Acts of the Apostles, the first Christians were known as people in 'the Way' – people en route, on the move, journeying. It became clear also that in the apostolic Church there was no sharp distinction between lay and ordained as well as considerable institutional fluidity and a great variety of ministries.[12] These various strands came together to unsettle previous ways of thinking about the Church, its nature and mission.

In contrast to the idea of the pilgrim people, the Church of England at the beginning of the twentieth century was decidedly institutional, hierarchical, bureaucratic and clerical. Its method of appointment (now as then), almost entirely the result of patronage, would be regarded as a form of corruption in every other area of life. The attempts to keep women from playing a role in the ordained ministry were viewed by non-believers as unseemly and unedifying, further proof, if proof were needed, of the inability of the Church to address any of the issues that concerned contemporary men and women in modern, democratic societies. In short, it was hard to imagine anything that looked less like the pilgrim people of God, which was deeply demoralizing for those paid to keep the institutional life of the Church going, who had embraced with enthusiasm the new ecclesiology of the Church as God's pilgrim people.

Church as priesthood

In the third place, the New Testament scholarship of the period also recovered what had been an important Reformation doctrine about the nature of the Church, namely that priesthood belonged to the whole community Jesus had established and not just the clergy. This was stated explicitly in the First Letter of Peter and was implicit almost everywhere else in the New Testament.[13] In 1 Peter the Christian community is called 'a chosen race, a royal priesthood, a holy nation, God's own people, in order that you may proclaim the mighty acts of him who called you out of darkness into his marvellous light'.[14] In the New Testament, the word priest is only used of the Jewish Temple priests and of Jesus himself, our great high priest; it is never used of Christian leaders. For this reason, at the Reformation, the Protestant churches generally preferred to call the clergy ministers or pastors rather than priests. The Church of England, however, retained the word 'priest' throughout the Book of Common Prayer (or 'Prayer Book'), including the ordination service contained within it. But the idea of the Church as the whole people of God raised anew the question of priesthood. In what sense is the Church as a whole a priesthood and in what sense can an ordained person be called priest? What, in other words, is priesthood?

In the ancient world priests were people whose function was to bridge the gap or overcome the barrier between God and people. For various reasons people felt estranged from God: they had sinned, they lacked any sense of God's presence with them, they could not discern God's will. At the time of Jesus people went to the priest because he could offer the sacrifices and make the offerings, while the High Priest alone was able to pass through the curtain into the holy of holies to perform the ritual of the Day of Atonement, all of which enabled people to draw near to God again. The priest reassured by making God real for people who felt distanced from him.

But the disciples found in Jesus the reassurance that priests gave, and found it more intensively. In the company of Jesus they experienced on the one hand the presence of God and his forgiveness (God was made real), and on the other a new vigour as the Spirit was also given to them and they became the people they were meant to be (*they* became real). Moreover, this did not end with his death. The presence of God was experienced even more powerfully after the Resurrection and Ascension when they met Jesus again as Spirit in their worship and fellowship: at the breaking of bread the presence of God was tangible. The only difference was that whereas in the days of his flesh Jesus was confined by the limitations of the body, as we all are, now he was available to all people in every place. What need had they, then, of Temple and priest? This was why the veil in the Temple that symbolized the separation of people from God was torn in two at the crucifixion: now that which previously depended on the hidden action of the few was available to all in Christian worship and fellowship. With the coming of Christ, the need for repeated sacrifice was abolished. Whenever Christians met together for worship and fellowship, God was made real and they became real. To meet the Church was to meet Christ, to find God, to have God made real. This was the Church's gift to the world and the heart of its mission. But making God possible is the fundamental priestly function. For this reason 1 Peter speaks of the entire Christian community – the many and not just the few – as a priesthood.

In what sense, then, could the Church continue to call some people priests when the whole baptized people of God, ordained and lay, is regarded in the New Testament as a priesthood? Obviously, the Church could not use the term priest in a way that suggested a return to the idea of the separate priestly tribe and the Temple priest: the priesthood of the many cannot be taken from them and placed into the hands of the few. We could not use the term priest in a way that undermines the fundamental New Testament principle, recovered at the Reformation, of the priesthood of all believers. This is a danger for churches that call their clergy priests, and the history of such churches has often been the history of a separate clerical caste, not simply distinct from, but over against the laity. We need to remember that the priesthood of the few derives from and only makes sense in the context of the priesthood of the many, of the whole Church. Ordained persons are priests because they focus in themselves and their office what belongs to the whole people of God. In this way, properly understood, priests serve to remind the whole Christian community of their priestly vocation while helping them to realize that priesthood. We can see how this works and is given expression in, for example, the Holy Communion service. Properly understood, the priest does not celebrate the Communion in the place of a laity who lack the power to celebrate. The Communion is celebrated by the whole people of God with the priest presiding – an understanding that was reinforced by moving the priest at the altar to a westward-facing position. (This is why so-called con-celebrations are really a nonsense. Every Communion is by its nature a con-celebration, of the whole community, though only one pair of hands can actually break the bread – those of the one who presides. Con-celebrations are really attempts at con-presidency – presidency by committee!) What the priest does on behalf of the whole people of God during the Communion service is to take and bless bread, thereby making something ordinary into a means of grace. This in turn inspires Christian people to see their daily life and work as priestly. In friendships, in family life, in secular work, in communities, day by day, it is the Christian's task so to live that each of these may become a channel of God's grace. This is the everyday reality of the priesthood of all believers. But this understanding of priest severely challenged some models of priesthood within the Church of England.

Church as leaven

In the fourth place, we might notice the way in which the task of the Church came to be differently conceived during the twentieth century as the focus shifted away from the need for individual salvation to a more generalized concern for human flourishing. In the nineteenth century the theological emphasis had been on the salvation of individual souls. Christians of all churches never doubted that the core of the Christian message was the offer of individual salvation: to be saved was to believe the gospel, and this gave priority and focus to the Church's mission as principally evangelistic. This was why so much effort and energy was expended in the Victorian period on foreign missions. Salvation depended on hearing and responding to the gospel. How could people in far-flung parts of the Empire hear if preachers were not prepared to go and preach?

In the twentieth century, the emphasis changed. On the one hand, there was a fresh appreciation of the relationship between salvation and eschatology (the end-time). Theology began to recover the Pauline idea that God's plan encompassed all creation and not just humanity. The redemption of the whole cosmos would not simply follow from a universal conversion to Christianity. God used the Church as one instrument of his redemptive work in the world; but it was not the only one. This suggested a more modest understanding of the significance and work of the Church and a shift in focus away from what the clergy did to what the laity alone could do in their secular callings. They had a vital part to play in making the kingdoms of this world more like the kingdom of Christ. The point was reinforced liturgically: the final prayer in the Rite A service of Holy Communion was said by everyone and contained the words, 'Send us out in the power of your Spirit to live and work to your praise and glory'.

On the other hand, the twentieth century saw a greater awareness of other world religions. Christians had to take other faiths into account and make a theological assessment that was not simply dismissive. Some Christians began to extend their idea of ecumenism to include them: perhaps Muslims, Hindus and Sikhs, present in the country now in substantial numbers, had also been granted glimpses of God and were also part of his purpose for the world. Some even suggested that good humanists might be 'anonymous Christians'.[15] The task of the Church, therefore, was not only to preach the gospel in order that others might become Christians; it was to work with all people of goodwill to build flourishing human communities, to be leaven in a diverse society.

Church as spiritual resource

The final significant change in the way the Church understood itself during the course of the twentieth century concerns the question of spirituality. Prior to this time, the Church would always have taken the view that to live a spiritual life required individuals to follow the spiritual paths laid down by the Church. Patterns of prayer, Bible reading, making confession, receiving the sacrament, going on retreat – in many different ways the different churches guided and managed the developing spiritual life of worshippers. Today the picture is very different. Just as in the National Health Service the assumption is that patients will take charge of their own health, so the Church is gradually, if reluctantly, coming to realize that people are taking responsibility for their own spiritual health, and the Church cannot dictate but only provide resources. Those who attended church regularly in the last decades of the twentieth century were doing so not as a result of any claims the Church might make about itself but because they found its religious resources spiritually nourishing. Similarly, those who walked away from regular attendance did so because they did not find regular Sunday worship resourcing them spiritually.

This has distressed those clergy who believed that the only way a religious commitment could show itself was by regular worship in a church. It would be understandable if some other new, more vibrant religion had appeared, challenging a venerable faith that had become weary and exhausted, unable to supply the spiritual resources people needed to meet new situations, reaching the end of its useful contribution to human development. Yet there was no obvious religious successor to Christianity taking its place in the way that Christianity once supplanted the pagan gods of the Roman Empire. Atheism is not a creed (though I will argue in the last chapter that there is a secular creed that must be taken seriously), and the most likely challenger of Christianity among other faiths, Islam, still has a long way to go before a successful 'Western' form emerges in the UK or Europe more generally. At the moment, conversion to Islam, as Kate Zebiri points out, means that British converts must repudiate almost every aspect of contemporary British culture – 'including materialism, consumerism, secularism, the sexualization of society, hedonism, individualism (to varying degrees) and familial disintegration'.[16] Although I think this is expressed rather negatively and is something of an exaggeration, it does point to the fact that Islam in its current cultural forms seems to offer little appeal to the broad mass of British people, and as a result there are no reports of conversions in any significant numbers. But if religion contributes something of great significance to life – as a focus of celebration or commemoration, as a source of meaning – one would expect the sudden loss of it to have some noticeable effects. What has happened?

The first thing to say is that leaving organized religion behind does not necessarily mean that Christianity has been immediately left behind. Some have been able to live on a Christian capital largely acquired in childhood without too much benefit of clergy. They have an outline understanding of the faith; they can recall some biblical passages, some helpful verses; they remember and can join in the more trad-itional hymns on BBC television's *Songs of Praise*; they can pray and recite the Lord's Prayer. However, this inheritance gets thinner with every passing year. Despite its legally protected status in the school syl-labus, religious education has not been able to stem the drift to religious illiteracy. There are many examples of that, but one of the most frequently cited illustrations is the millennial exhibition on Christian art, called Seeing Salvation, held in the National Gallery in 2000. The Director, Neil McGregor, brought together a magnificent collection of art and artefacts encompassing two thousand years of Christian history. Very large numbers of people came to the gallery. Some Christian com-mentators hailed this as evidence of continuing interest in the Christian faith – which was no doubt true. However, of even greater cultural significance was probably the Director's decision to produce a catalogue that not only explained the exhibits in historical and artistic terms, but also attempted to give a theological account of their meaning. Presumably, this was thought necessary because the people who came had begun to lose the religious references. In other words, the exhibition pointed to the danger of the times – that if people assume that leaving organized religion will not erode spiritual resources, they are mistaken. But it is the kind of mistake that does not show itself until it is late in the day, perhaps even too late.

It is also possible that in abandoning organized Christianity – the Church – people have not abandoned religion altogether, or more precisely, spirituality. It is now widely argued by some scholars that this is precisely what has happened: organized religion is in process of giving way to alternative forms of small-group spirituality.[17] It has been pointed out how often in recent years there have been people who want to oppose 'spirituality' to (organized or institutional) 'religion'. The American sociologist of religion, Wade Clark Roof, quotes someone he once interviewed who enables us to see what is at issue:

Spirituality, I think, is what enters you and lifts you up and moves you to be a better person, a more open person. I don't think religion does that. Religion tells you what to do and when to do it, when to kneel, when to stand up, all of that stuff. Lots of rules.[18]

Alternative spiritualities are seen as helpful in the search for one's own authentic spirituality. Religion wants to dictate what form everyone's spirituality should take – hence the imposition of norms and rules and patterns of behaviour. The newer types of spirituality – some of which are called New Age – are about exploration and quest.

This was the thesis put forward by a group of academics from Lancaster University following research in the small English market town of Kendal between 2000 and 2002. They found 53 small groups practising forms of holistic spirituality in and around Kendal. The groups included: yoga, circle dancing, reiki, Sai Baba groups, Shiatsu, Psychic Consultancy, Universal Peace dancing groups, Green Spirit groups – the list goes on.[19] If this were happening in a small town in Cumbria, far from the presumed more culturally progressive urban centres, it probably indicated trends that were nationwide. On the basis of what the researchers found, they concluded that while organized religion was in what looked like terminal decline (with the exception of the more charismatic evangelicals), alternative groups were growing in popularity. They predicted that in numerical terms, those in holistic spirituality groups would exceed those in Christian churches sometime after 2040 – a time roughly after the researchers would all be dead!

How true is this argument? There are a number of reasons for being cautious. First, it is by no means obvious that the undoubted shift from accepting what is laid down – traditional religion – to wanting to plot one's own spiritual path leads inevitably to some New Age type of spirituality or the rejection of the Church. People may indeed want to explore and discover for themselves, and they may want to do that in a small group, but they may pursue their quest and still find traditional forms of Christianity helpful or even essential. There is evidence that many are doing just this, possibly more people than are involved in alternative spiritualities. Three examples will serve to make the point: Taizé, the Alpha course and house groups.

The Taizé community had its origins in an attempt by a Swiss Protestant, Roger Louis Schutz-Marsauche, to offer shelter to political refugees, including Jews, in the semi-derelict village of Taizé in east-central France at the start of the Second World War. Brother Roger (as he was later known) began keeping a regular pattern of daily prayer in which his visitors and guests would join. This was no doubt inspired by the nearby ruins of Cluny Abbey, a significant medieval Benedictine monastery. After the war, in 1949, he established something unique – an ecumenical monastery – that attracted young men from many traditions and nationalities into the community. Taizé has since developed into one of the world's most important centres of pilgrimage, drawing young people in particular from every country on the planet, whether members of churches or not. Today, up to 5,000 young people make their way to Taizé each week to take part in the prayer and work of the community, which now numbers almost one hundred. Brother Roger himself was brutally stabbed to death in front of 2,500 people during a service there in 2005. The work has since continued under his successor, Brother Alois, a Roman Catholic.

At the heart of Taizé are the three daily services in the monastic tradition – a mix of Scripture reading, prayer and singing, interspersed with substantial periods of silence and meditation – followed by Bible study and discussion in small groups.

Taizé is interesting because it bears out the first part of the thesis that in contemporary culture many, if not most, young people still pursue spiritual concerns, but want to do so in small groups, through journeys of self-discovery and personal exploration, and not through some pattern of spirituality prescribed by the Church that you either take or leave. However, these thousands of young people contradict the idea that such a pattern of personal exploration is incompatible with, or cannot be accommodated within, or leads to the rejection of, forms of organized Christianity. The time of silence and contemplation, the small groups and the community's concern for the world's poor, enable young seekers to explore faith and its implications for living in the modern world and also to 'taste and see that the LORD is good'.[20] The challenge for the churches is to enable and encourage the development of similar centres in the UK.

A second example would be the Alpha courses. These courses began at Holy Trinity Church, Brompton, in the 1980s, as an attempt by an Anglican evangelical church to influence new generations of young adults who seemed to know little of the Christian faith. Since then, and particularly since 1990 when the Revd Nicky Gumbel was put in charge, Alpha courses have spread across the world into some 163 countries and have been taken up by almost every major Christian denomination. The casual observer might think that the course is very prescriptive in that it follows a definite outline of topics and, therefore, is an example of organized religion rather than spirituality for seekers (those who wish to use the Alpha brand have to abide by strict conditions). There is some truth in this. However, Alpha works by inviting attenders to be open and exploratory. The Holy Trinity website says this about Alpha:

Who is Alpha for?

Alpha is for everyone; no question is out of bounds and you are free to discuss as much or as little as you wish. We don't assume any background knowledge of or belief in Christianity and everyone is welcome.

What is Alpha?

Alpha is an opportunity to explore the meaning of life in an informal, fun and friendly environment. The Alpha course consists of a series of talks, looking at topics including 'Who is Jesus?' and 'Why and how do I pray?' with the option of a weekend away. We meet for supper and each talk is followed by discussion in small groups.[21]

This formula for encouraging people to engage afresh or for the first time with Christianity is one of the few that has proved successful in contemporary society. Like Taizé, it responds to the culture of the times.

Finally, we might notice the way in which all the churches have encouraged various forms of house group. Some churches have organized themselves completely as a house church, arguing that this is being faithful to the New Testament. Other Christians have met this way in countries where either Christianity or all religions are discouraged – certain Islamic countries, China, Vietnam and so on. In Britain, many evangelical churches encourage their members to meet in homes mid-week on a regular basis, as a way of giving people the pastoral support that is only possible on a more intimate basis. Most denominations offer small group meetings for prayer, study or fellowship at some time during the year.

But is it true that the loss of Christianity has had or is having no consequences? Many commentators have remarked on the way younger generations – people in their thirties or forties – have been responding to modern society and culture. Despite the prosperity – that is, the continually rising prosperity of the period up to the global financial crisis that began in late 2008; despite the opportunities to pursue careers, take holidays, exercise personal choices over a whole range of life's activities, many have continued to wonder whether there is not more to life. Is this all the good life amounts to? Is there nothing more satisfying than this? Is the meaning of my life to be exhaustively defined by my achievements, such as they are, in areas like family, career, personal wealth and material well-being? This would not be the first time in history that such questions have been asked. In the past, however, it has often resulted in a return to religion, and often involved whole classes of people. The rise of Methodism in the eighteenth century – wholly unpredicted – would be one example. If we are to understand contemporary indifference towards the Church we have to take seriously the possibility that the Christianity that is offered has been found wanting. It no longer helps people navigate their way through life's ups and downs. This raises a serious and urgent question about the ability or willingness of the Church, its theologians and ministers, to engage with contemporary culture and the questions people face today. Many people have clearly turned away in sorrow and regret. Some have found spiritual resources outside organized religion with alternative spiritualities. Most have not, but fall back on this inherited Christian capital that is not being renewed. The significance of Taizé and Alpha lies here – they recognize that the Church has a continuing role to play as a spiritual resource where many continue to find the institutional Church in its local incarnation is not for them. There is also the recognition that 'private' or 'personal' spiritual experience is not something that occurs prior to or independently of some living spiritual tradition. The spiritual experiences we individually have are profoundly influenced and shaped by particular religious traditions. Spirituality is born out of the conversation that goes on all the time within a tradition. There cannot be a conversation of one.

What is ministry?

Before we leave these theological considerations, something needs to be said about the idea of ministry itself, and then ordained ministry. There have been changes here during the twentieth century as well.

One of the difficulties in any discussion of ministry is that the word is used in a number of different ways. We need to distinguish between them.

All-member ministry?

In recent years it has become fashionable to talk more and more about everyone in the Church having a ministry by virtue of their baptism – all-member ministry. There are two problems with this way of speaking. In the first place, the notion of ministry is made to resemble some capacious bag into which everything can be made to fit. But if everyone has a ministry and everything they do is ministry, it is hard to formulate a coherent definition of what ministry is and, crucially, is not. Then in the second place, speaking of the ministry that all have as a result of baptism assumes that everyone who attends church is indeed baptized and does so as a fully committed and fully energized member. (I leave aside the fact that some Christians do not have sacraments at all – such

as the Quakers and the Salvation Army.) The reality in most congregations is that there is a range of commitment, capabilities, concerns and
energy. Although division by de Lubac (see page 37) of congregations
into active and passive, ordained and lay, will not do, it does make the
point that there are differences between people within congregations:
some are exercising a ministry and some are receiving. Perhaps we need
to distinguish between 'vocation' and 'ministry'. Both words have been
hijacked and used exclusively of the clergy in the past and both need
recovering, but it is often the idea of vocation rather than ministry that
seems to lie behind much talk of ministry today.

The concept of 'vocation' (or calling) has often been used in the past,
and sometimes today, in a rather narrow sense to mean the call to
ordained ministry, or one of the caring professions, such as teaching or
nursing, where people may be motivated by something other than the
need to earn a wage and where the material rewards are probably not
great in any case. But it has also been used in a more expanded sense
to mean any of the roles that a Christian might undertake. This was
what Martin Luther meant by vocation. He taught that women and men
were called by God to their secular work, rejecting any suggestion that
ordination was a higher or holier calling. He also believed that Christians were not only called in their occupations – as butcher, baker or
candlestick-maker – but also in their domestic roles as husband or
wife, mother or father. A calling does not take you out of the world but
brings you to service in the world. As he himself said in a sermon,
'If everyone serves his neighbour; then the world would be full of
worship.'[22] All Christians have a vocation. Indeed, they might have
several. But having a vocation is not the same as having a ministry –
though some people's vocation will be the call to ministry.

The ministry of the Church

We are on safer ground if we begin by recognizing first that the Church
as a corporate body has a ministry: it seeks to share in Christ's ministry
to the world. Christ's ministry was to demonstrate the reign of God in
word and deed. Christ began his ministry with the call to repentance
in the face of the coming reign (or kingdom) of God. He then taught
about the nature of that reign, most memorably in parables but also in
mighty deeds of feeding, healing and forgiving. The Church participates
in this ministry of proclaiming and enacting the kingdom of God through
its preaching and teaching, in the celebration of the sacraments and in
pastoral work. Many, both ordained and lay, contribute to and share in
this ministry; individual members of the Church are given a variety of
gifts by the one Holy Spirit to enable that to happen. But within each
congregation some, and not others, are asked to use the particular gifts

they are given to undertake specific tasks for 'the common good' and to build up the body.[23] This is ministry. In turn, this ministry enables lay Christians to fulfil their particular vocations (or apostolate)[24] in the secular world of employment, family and community life.

Ordained ministry

Some are called to exercise leadership roles in ministry on behalf of the Christian community as a whole, for all groups need leadership. Those who do so are selected, trained and set apart or commissioned for this task by the Church. They are not self-selecting or self-appointed. The Church has commissioned people for various tasks and in various ways throughout its history. Ordained ministry has been one of these commissioned ministries.

In broad terms, as we said in the introduction, the task of the clergy is to support the mission of the Church in making God possible, making God findable. This works itself out with a twofold focus. First, the clergy are charged with ministering in and to their congregations. They must ensure that the body of Christ is built up. They do not work alone in this, though they may have particular functions that others do not share, such as presiding at the Eucharist or pronouncing absolution. But it is their responsibility to see that this work of building up the people of God goes on. In the second place they have a representative role. They stand for the Christian Church in the wider community (which is one reason why they wear distinctive dress). This is why a hospital visit by the clergy is regarded as a visit from 'the Church' whereas a visit by a lay person is viewed as an act of personal kindness and Christian charity. This is not to deny that all Christians in some sense represent their Church; but clergy are commissioned to be the visible focus of the local congregation and to speak and act on its behalf in the wider community. Lay people may have opportunities to witness to God in their day-to-day lives; clergy, by their very presence, speak of a spiritual dimension in life. Clergy are also thought to be interested in the well-being of all people, not simply their own congregation, and because of that their representative role may become even broader: they may be seen as representing the interests of all people in a particular locality. It is in this representative capacity that a priest may be asked to be a school governor or to serve on this committee or with that charitable trust or to take a memorial service. The way these two functions – ministering to the congregation and ministering in the parish – are worked out changes as circumstances change, as the following chapters will seek to show. But all clergy have to strike some sort of balance between them. If priests spent all their time with their congregation they would lose touch with that wider world in which their members have to live out their lives and for which they want encouragement and counsel. Conversely, if they spent all their time with non-members and secular organizations they would lose the confidence of lay members of congregations.[25]

Conclusion

The role of the clergy in the twentieth century was, then, profoundly affected not only by changes in theology, especially ecclesiology, but also by cultural shifts. Indeed, the theological changes were often as much the result of circumstance forcing theological reassessment as they were of any theological development uninfluenced by external factors. Either way, changes in theology as well as circumstance over the past 50 or so years have profound implications for ministry.

In this chapter I have spoken of five changes in the way the Church came to understand itself. But these changes have taken place at a time when there has been a further challenge to the Church that may turn out to be of greater significance than these five. I refer to the shift that has taken place in people's attitude towards authority. Europe in the modern period has been torn apart by two prolonged bouts of revolution, civil war, national and international conflict, persecutions and pogroms. The driving force of the first was religious difference and convulsed the first half of the seventeenth century. It ended with the Peace of Westphalia in 1648 and the historic decision to live with religious difference, Protestant and Catholic. The second round of conflict was ideologically driven as democracy fought totalitarianism of both the right (Fascism) and the left (Communism). It ended first with the defeat of Nazi Germany in 1945 and then with the collapse of Communism in 1989. But the two periods left Europeans profoundly suspicious of ideologies, whether religious or political, and attempts to frame some all-encompassing theory that explains all knowledge and experience (a grand narrative), such as Christianity or Communism. The European experience of such grand narratives was that they were attempts to support some or other power structure – the Church, the Party and so forth. Europeans came to experience and then to value diversity and choice; they were increasingly sceptical about claims by any political or religious creed to be able to explain all human experience and human destiny.

In religion, this resulted in people becoming increasingly their own authority. I referred to this in the previous chapter as 'the democratization of religion'. In other words, people are making up their own minds about what they believe, how they live, which denomination they belong to, and react badly to anything that suggests they can be told what to think or how to act. We see that most powerfully (and paradoxically) illustrated in the refusal of Roman Catholics across the Western world to abide by that church's teaching on contraception, despite, presumably, their belief that the Roman Catholic Church's pronouncements reflected the mind of Christ. Many worshippers might be Roman Catholic at Sunday mass but they are decidedly Protestant the rest of the time. A libertarian genie was released in the second half of the twentieth century that will not now be put back in the bottle. The Church has found this aspect of contemporary culture and society very difficult to know how to handle.

The low morale that afflicts some clergy in the Western world in these first years of the third Christian millennium is, therefore, symptomatic of wider anxieties about the role of the Church in the emerging culture of post-Christian society. The models of ministry that influence how clergy see themselves, and that guide them in their day-to-day work, are beginning to need substantial modification in the light of these cultural changes. New models of ordained ministry can only emerge if we are willing to admit the inadequacy of existing models and the need for change.

In Part 2 I will look at four models of ministry that have shaped Anglican ministry in the past and continue to exercise an influence in the present. I begin with what I call the 'classical' model – the model that we find commended by George Herbert in the seventeenth century and that has arguably been the most influential in subsequent Anglican history. We then consider two types that have their origins in two quite different parts of the Anglican spectrum of theology and ecclesiology – the evangelical and the catholic (Anglo-Catholic). Finally I turn to a model that has been drawn on increasingly in the latter half of the twentieth century: the 'utility' model of social activism and personal therapy. In each case I will seek to evaluate the model, asking how far it has a continuing relevance and how far it needs to be re-envisioned or discarded.

Part 2
MODELS OF MINISTRY

3

Classical: the parson

———◆———

When I mention religion I mean the Christian religion; and not
only the Christian religion, but the Protestant religion; and not only
the Protestant religion, but the Church of England.
Parson Thwackum in Henry Fielding, Tom Jones, *1749*

Origins and evolution

In 1652, a small book was published, some twenty years after the author
died, that provided a model for Anglican ordained ministry until well
into the twentieth century. It was still warmly commended in the theological college where I trained in the late 1960s, though in more recent
years it has often been identified as an unhelpful model in the modern
context.[1] George Herbert (1593–1633) had written *The Country Parson:
His Character and Rule of Holy Life* after abandoning an academic and
political career for marriage and ordination. He married Jane Danvers
in 1629 and a year later became rector of the rural parishes of Fugglestone
St Peter and Bemerton St Andrew in the Diocese of Salisbury. But in
1633 he died in his rectory, leaving his manuscript for others to publish.
In a few short chapters Herbert set out his understanding of the calling
and responsibilities of a clergyman of the Church of England. He wrote
to provide himself with a 'Mark to aim at'.[2] In the event, both in his
own life and through his book, he set a pattern for other clergy to follow, a benchmark against which all subsequent generations of Anglican
clergy until comparatively recently would judge their own ministries.[3]
The book was especially influential because, until the Victorian period,
Anglican clergy received no formal training and even as late as 1907
half of those ordained had never spent any time in a theological college.
They learnt by observation and what they could glean from manuals of
best practice.[4] (As residential training becomes unaffordable for all, the
era of the theological college may turn out to have been quite short
and now near its end.)

What Herbert described is the life and work of an ordained minister
according to the Book of Common Prayer.[5] Herbert wrote at what was
a defining moment for Anglicanism. The Church was involved in sharp

theological controversy between those – we can call them 'inclusivists' – who wanted the Church of England to be able to welcome within it a considerable range of theological opinion (for diversity was the reality of post-Reformation Christianity in England), and the Puritans who favoured more tightly drawn theological boundaries – we can call these the 'exclusivists'. The inclusive thinking that we encounter in Herbert's book prevailed, though exclusivist arguments have resurfaced from time to time in the national Church, not least in recent years.

As well as the more explicit references to the work of a priest in the ordination service, the Prayer Book makes a number of other assumptions about ordained ministry and the Church. Herbert draws out and explores these in his handbook. The main assumptions and themes are these:

1 The Anglican priest is a minister of a national (established) Church that is charged with the task of making a nominally Christian nation into a Christian commonwealth.
2 The primary responsibility of the priest is to teach and expound the word of God, which is the sole authority in matters of faith.
3 The priest is pastor to all who live within his parish boundaries and this requires him to be sensitive to their needs by residing in the parish; he is a known person, a *persona*, the parson.

This produced a distinctive Anglican ecclesiology and ethos, what we might call the classical model of the Anglican parson – the men who inhabit so much of English literature in the novels of Henry Fielding, Jane Austen, Anthony Trollope and George Orwell.[6] Let us examine each of these assumptions in turn.

The model

A national Church

At the Reformation, the Church *in* England became the Church *of* England, established by Parliament. The sovereign, not the Pope, became its Supreme Governor. This proved a mixed blessing for the mission of the Church.

On the one hand, the freedom that came with the break from Rome after 1533–4 enabled the Church of England to produce a Prayer Book and a Bible in a language that ordinary people could understand. Archbishop Thomas Cranmer's Prayer Book (1549 – which used Miles Coverdale's translation of Scripture) and the later King James Bible, or Authorized Version, in English (1611) were a great gain for the Christian mission: they became two of the greatest spiritual resources the Christian

Church has ever produced in the English-speaking world. Generations of people have had their spiritual lives nourished as they learnt by heart collects from the Prayer Book and passages from the Authorized Version of the Bible; and in learning to say the Catechism (included by Cranmer in the first Prayer Book of 1549) and the Litany, they learnt how to think and behave as Christians in the world.

Establishment, especially under Elizabeth I (the Elizabethan Settlement), also meant that for reasons of state as well as religion, the national Church sought to be a *via media* between Rome (catholic Christianity) and Geneva (reformed Christianity). This gave the Church of England a certain doctrinal stance: it would retain a respect for the past by not abandoning its catholic inheritance (including episcopacy), but it would reform it. As we have already noted, this attempt to steer a middle course was severely tested in the seventeenth century by the Puritans, who wanted to make the Church more Protestant, but the work and witness of the Caroline (living during the reigns of Kings Charles I and II) divines – Lancelot Andrewes, William Laud, Jeremy Taylor, Thomas Ken – ensured that the catholic inheritance was not lost. The Church of England took a middle path between continental Calvinism and Roman Catholicism. The Church was catholic but reformed, and consciously sought to be a broad Church embracing a range of theological opinions. This has bequeathed to the contemporary Church of England a continuing willingness to tolerate a wide range of views and liturgical styles. The instincts of the Anglican Church and its ordained ministry have historically been towards inclusion.

The close association with the crown and government also gave the Church over the years unique opportunities to influence the direction of national life and government policy as it stood alongside government in 'critical solidarity'. The task of the Church was not to call men and women out of the secular world but to equip them for service in it. The task of the laity was to make the kingdom of this world more like the kingdom of Christ. Many monarchs and prime ministers – though by no means all – accepted their role as a Christian vocation. Before the democratic reforms of the nineteenth century, the bishops wielded a certain amount of real power through their membership of the House of Lords. That has now disappeared, leaving them with a little influence but no power.

The concept of a national Church has meant above all that from its inception the Church of England accepted that it had a pastoral responsibility towards all the people of England and not just regular attenders, towards every aspect of life and not just church life, and towards all the institutions of the state. Apologists for the establishment of the Church of England would say that this was because at both national and local level the Church was committed to a 'community' and not an 'associational' understanding of what it is to be the Church. In other words, it did not choose to make too hard and fast a distinction between those who were 'true believers' and those who were not. It sought to be as inclusive as possible by being chaplain to the nation. Consequently, the edges of the Anglican Church have never been tightly circumscribed – and most Anglicans saw this as a strength.

On the other hand, the idea of a national Church also resulted in undoubted losses. To some extent, for example, it lost the sense of being part of a universal Church. It is one of the abiding strengths of the Roman Catholic Church that it is to be found in almost every part of the world: it is catholic in the sense of being universally present, and its members have a sense of belonging to a world-wide Church. The Church of England sought to think of itself as part of the universal Church of Christ, but this seemed an insubstantial claim compared with Roman Catholicism, which had such a universal reach. However, the development of the British Empire led to the growth of the world-wide Anglican communion (really from the late eighteenth century), and in more recent times there has been a mutual recognition of the ministries of the Anglican and some mainly North European churches – such as the Evangelical-Lutheran churches of Norway, Sweden and Finland – in the Porvoo communion.[7] But the reality is that the Anglican Church was and remains primarily a relatively small, mainly English-speaking denomination on the world stage. This becomes increasingly an issue for contemporary practising Anglican lay people as their jobs and vacations take them to other countries and they look for churches in their tradition.

But establishment comes at a price. The Church has to tread a fine and careful line between being supportive of government and being merely subordinate. Governments are happy to have the Church's prayers but less keen to receive its prophetic word.

Expounding the word of God

The break with Rome was essentially about two things: How was salvation to be secured? Where did authority in matters of doctrine and church order lie? For the reformers, the Bible provided the answer to both questions. Salvation came through faith in Jesus Christ, who is known only through Holy Scripture. Final authority in matters of faith and practice likewise lay with the Bible. The Church of England taught that its own authority derived from the Scriptures and that what it taught and practised was subject to them. But the Scriptures do not interpret themselves, and a careful reading of the Thirty-Nine Articles of Religion makes it clear that the reformers recognized this; reason has a part to play:

Holy Scripture containeth all things necessary to salvation: so that whatsoever is not read therein, *nor may be proved thereby*, is not required of any man, that it should be believed as an article of the Faith, or be thought requisite or necessary to salvation.[8]

While reason may not lead us to contradict Scripture (Article XX), it is necessary to interpret and apply – or 'prove' – Scripture (Article VI). The centrality of Scripture and the need to expound it became one of the principal differences between the catholic (unreformed) and the reformed Church. The reformed priest had to be a preacher, an expounder of the word of God. Indeed, the term 'preacher' came to be used of priests, and until the catholic revival of the nineteenth century the pulpit was often the dominant piece of furniture in Anglican churches.

All of this pointed towards the need for an educated priesthood. The skills required of the priest in the medieval Church were minimal: an ability to break a piece of bread and recite the words of the mass (albeit in a strange tongue – Latin). As a result, most pre-Reformation priests were poor men with little education. But preaching and teaching from the Scriptures necessitated a literate clergy. In this respect the Church of England stood in the Protestant tradition. The Roman Catholic Church could survive with mass priests and the occasional sermon from a member of a preaching order, but Protestants were fed each week by the interpreted word as much as by broken bread. Herbert exhorted the clergy to bless God in prayer after each sermon using these words:

And now Lord, thou hast fed us with the bread of life: so man did eat Angel's food: Oh, Lord, bless it: Oh Lord make it health and strength unto us; still striving and prospering so long within us, until our obedience reach the measure of thy love, who hast done for us as much as may be.[9]

For this reason Herbert said that the country parson should preach 'constantly', only stopping for serious illness. The pulpit was his 'joy and his throne'.[10]

This is not to say that the ideal was always achieved. In the immediate aftermath of the Reformation the clergy had to be provided with a Book of Homilies from which they could read sermons on Sundays because they were unused to writing them, and in the eighteenth century, when clergy brought an hourglass into the pulpit to ensure that the congregation had a full 60 minutes, the preacher might read from a book rather than compose his own. (Books of sermons were printed to look like handwritten manuscripts for this reason – as we can see in a well-known Hogarth cartoon, *Sleeping Congregation*.) But in general the preparation and delivery of sermons has always been seen as an important part of an Anglican priest's task. For Anglican evangelicals it was and remains central.

The style of preaching was also important. Herbert objected to the Puritan habit of 'crumbling' the text – breaking it down phrase by phrase or even word by word. This was to treat the Scriptures as if they were a 'dictionary'.[11] People needed to become familiar with substantial texts and have whole passages expounded. ('Crumbling' is still practised in some contemporary evangelical preaching.)

The emphasis on the word was also an incentive to improve the educational standards of the people. It is often said that when missionaries went to Africa in the nineteenth century, Roman Catholics built clinics while Protestants built schools. Hearing the Scriptures read in the vernacular in church was good, but having a laity who could read the Bible for themselves was better. Even so, the laity would need competent clergy who could act as guides and mentors in the process of becoming familiar with the Scriptures, their meaning and application. (Some would argue that all the Reformation did was replace one type of authoritarian ministry with another; that the new presbyter was but the old priest writ large.[12])

One important way in which the clergy fulfilled their task of inducting the rising generation into the Christian faith was through the Catechism. This was part of the Prayer Book and consisted of a number of questions and answers on key points of Christian teaching to be committed to memory before confirmation. It included the Creed, the Ten Commandments and the Lord's Prayer. The children of each parish would be tested on what they had learnt by the parish priest during evening prayer. It was still in use in Anglican parishes as late as the 1950s. It formed the basis of my own preparation for confirmation as a child in 1953. I was particularly grateful for some of its careful explanations of doctrine – such as the definition of a sacrament as 'an outward and visible sign of an inward and spiritual grace' – and remember them to this day. However, the Catechism was also a means of social control, as the response to the question, 'What is thy duty towards thy Neighbour?' reveals. The child answered that he must love his neighbour 'as myself, and to do to all men, as I would they should do unto me: To love, honour, and succour my father and mother', but also:

> To honour and obey the King, and all that are put in authority under him: To submit myself to all my governors, teachers and spiritual pastors and masters: To order myself lowly and reverently to all my betters ... Not to covet nor desire other men's goods; but to learn and labour truly to get mine own living, and to do my duty in that state of life, unto which it shall please God to call me.[13]

'That state of life, unto which it shall please God to call me' was a way of keeping the lower orders and women in their place, squashing all ambition and aspiration.

The resident priest

George Herbert wrote his manual for clergy in a parochially organized Church. He insisted that Anglican priests should be resident in their parishes. This may seem an uncontroversial matter now, but the parish system has frequently been called into question, and residence was the exception rather than the rule for much of Anglican history. The parochial system was the principal means by which the Church of England gave effect at local level to its foundational assumptions about the nature of the Church and its mission: that every parishioner, whether an active member of the Church or not, was a proper object of the Church's concern; and that a large part of the clergyman's role could only be realized if he were fully involved in the secular life of the parish. Both of these assumptions have been and still are challenged.

The Elizabethan Settlement of 1559 took it for granted that everyone living in England was a member both of the nation and the established Church. Richard Hooker, as noted in the previous chapter, famously wrote in his *Of the Laws of Ecclesiastical Polity* (1594) that there was not a member of the commonwealth who was not a member of the Church of England nor a member of the Church of England who was not a member of the commonwealth.[14] All people were Anglican by birth. This was a sentiment that made more sense then than now: the numbers of non-believers and Roman Catholics was comparatively small and the Anglican Church sought to hold within itself a broad range of Protestant theological positions. But tensions were always there between those who favoured a Church that was open to a variety of Christian opinion and those who believed the Church could only ever be a gathered community of one opinion. These particular tensions, always just below the surface, have appeared again in recent years as a result of debates about baptism policy and evangelism. But in the sixteenth and early seventeenth centuries, when the role of the parish priest was crucially being fashioned, the view that all parishioners were the responsibility of the rector or vicar of the parish finally prevailed.

In Herbert's day, and until the nineteenth century, the problem of non-residence could be acute. For a variety of reasons, clergy did not live in their parishes. Sometimes greed led a man to acquire more than one living – a pre-reformation abuse that was not corrected by the reformers. More often it was not greed but poverty that drove a man to secure several stipends. Occasionally, clergy simply did not like one or other of their parishes and so rarely visited. The services of the church were kept going by non-beneficed clergy, of whom there were large numbers. They rode to the churches of the vicars that employed them to say matins or evensong and perhaps to stay on and marry, baptize or bury people – for a fee. The departure of the unbeneficed clergy on horseback over Magdalen Bridge in Oxford each Sunday morning became a familiar sight. Herbert realized that such a freelance approach to ministry was far from ideal. Clergy should live in their parishes. 'I sat daily with you teaching in the Temple' is a text he quotes in support of this. But it was only by legislation in the Victorian period that the Church finally ensured that all beneficed clergy lived in their parishes; until then there was only the power of persuasion and example.

The reason for residence is not hard to see, for if the priest was to discharge the duties laid upon him at ordination he would need to be actively engaged with not just his congregation but all parishioners on a daily basis. According to the Prayer Book's service for the ordination of a priest, the priest was:

> to teach, and to premonish, to feed and provide for the Lord's family; to seek for Christ's sheep that are dispersed abroad, and for his children who are in the midst of this naughty world, that they may be saved through Christ for ever.[15]

However this was interpreted, it required regular and proactive contact with congregation and parishioners. Herbert recommended regular visiting of the parish by 'quarters' as a way of carrying out this mandate:

> The Country Parson upon the afternoons in the weekdays, takes occasion sometimes to visit in person, now one quarter of his Parish, now another. For there he shall find his flock most naturally as they are, wallowing in the midst of their affairs ...[16]

The priest also had a duty to read morning and evening prayer and, according to a rubric from the Prayer Book, 'shall cause a Bell to be tolled thereunto a convenient time before he begin, that the people may come to hear God's word, and to pray with him'. That too required residence. George Herbert discharged this particular duty assiduously, beginning with his own household. Izaak Walton noted that most of his parishioners and 'many gentlemen in the neighbourhood' came to say their prayers twice each day, while 'some of the meaner sort' so loved and respected their priest that 'they would let the plough rest when Mr Herbert's Saints Bell rang to prayers, that they might also offer their devotions to God with him; and would then return back to their plough'.[17]

In the present context, residence is also important if the priest is to be able to use, say, the Church's liturgies in pastorally effective ways.

Anglican priests still baptize about 20 per cent of all children, officiate at about one third of all marriages and conduct the funerals of the majority of people. They generally perform these occasional offices well because they know something of the local situation and because they have developed a liturgical style that is sensitive to the needs of mixed congregations of believers and unbelievers. Wesley Carr, a former Dean of Westminster Abbey, has described this as an 'interpretive ministry'.[18] It is a quite different ministry from that of, for example, the Roman Catholic priest who is pastor to the Roman Catholic community, whether practising or lapsed. But in the twenty-first century, the absentee vicar is once again a reality in many areas of the country due to the fall in numbers of clergy, the creation of multiple benefices and the cost of maintaining stipendiary ministry at previous levels.

But residence was also necessary because the priest was regarded as the principal agent of God's work in the parish. The assumption of the Prayer Book is that pastoral work as well as the governance and liturgical leadership of the church lies with the priest. Each of these assumptions came to be challenged in the modern period. The rise of more democratic forms of secular government was followed by demands in the Church for more democratic structures, culminating in the twentieth century with synodical government. A more educated laity began to share the leading of worship. The pastoral role of the clergy was progressively weakened as the welfare state developed after the Second World War.

Summarizing, we can say that this classical model of the Anglican priest served the Prayer Book understanding of the role of the Church of England as the national Church. The parson would practise an inclusive ministry to all in his parish. Above all, he would seek to make God findable through the patient expounding of the word, bringing Scripture to bear on the issues that concerned people in their day-to-day lives. But how did this work itself out?

The model in practice

Church decline in the Hanoverian period

During the eighteenth century, the Anglican ministry went into something of a decline. This was the Age of Reason, when emotion was suspect and what was preached had to pass the test of reasonableness. The Church's best preachers and apologists did offer a robust defence of Christianity (in some contrast to their counterparts in France), but on the whole the result was a Church that was worthy but dull, prone to dispense good advice rather than good news. Sermons tended to be rather lengthy ethical treatises topped and tailed with biblical quotations, rather than expositions of Scripture. It was a style that disturbed the evangelicals. The sacrament of Holy Communion was celebrated infrequently – which concerned the Anglo-Catholics in the following century – and church buildings were often allowed to fall into a state of disrepair. In addition, clergy holding appointments in several parishes resulted in, as we saw above in relation to Herbert's day, widespread non-residence and the liturgical and pastoral work of the church being undertaken by 'curates' – unbeneficed and often quite poor clergy who were employed by the absentee vicar to take Sunday services and the occasional offices. This is not to deny that there were some, perhaps many, conscientious bishops and clergy; but on the whole, and not surprisingly, there was little love lost between clergy and people in Hanoverian England. Little wonder that the Methodists – who at first tried to revive the national Church from within – eventually felt they could not maintain a home in the Church of England and had to leave.

Socially useful clergy

England remained largely rural until the later nineteenth century. This was the ideal context for both the Prayer Book and Herbert's model. In the life of such communities, Anglican parsons played a central role, being valued for their religious function and also for wider social roles they undertook. For as well as conducting Sunday services, baptizing, marrying and burying their parishioners (surplice duties) and, crucially, keeping records of these events, they also performed many other social functions. Anthony Russell, in a study of clerical handbooks published between 1750 and 1875, has listed these additional tasks.[19]

So, for example, clergy were dispensers of charity. The ordinal required deacons to 'search for the sick, poor and impotent people in the parish' with a view to relieving their distress. This might be done through the more formal channels of the poor law and the local rates, or it might be done less formally through the alms of parishioners (collected at Holy Communion), from the income of charitable trusts or from the donations of wealthy gentry. While the reforms of the Victorian period removed the rate-borne relief of poverty from the hands of the clergy, there remained an expectation for a long time that the clergy would always be an alternative source of some help for those most in need. (Herbert spoke of charity as 'a hook' to win people for God, but the Evangelicals and Anglo-Catholics urged clergy not to involve themselves directly in poor relief in case they came to be valued for their material at the expense of their spiritual role.)[20]

Clergy were also involved in law and order in a variety of ways – because they believed they had a concern for people's morals as well as religion. They enforced the penalties laid down by church courts in such matters as blasphemy, bastardy and fornication. Parson Woodforde records in his diary for 3 February, 1768, how Sarah Gore was sent by the court at Wells to his church to make public confession of her sin in having a child out of wedlock. In the nineteenth century these functions were gradually transferred to civil courts. In addition, many clergy were magistrates. The parish priest of Sheffield in the 1850s was the city's chief magistrate. His Monday mornings would be spent sentencing those parishioners who had been involved in Chartist riots, petty thefts or drunken brawls over the weekend. But the bishops became increasingly anxious about clergy in these roles and the practice of clerical justices began to die away.

Clergy ran schools and taught in them. In the early nineteenth century the Church School was considered to be a key part of the Church's evangelistic strategy. By 1851, Anglican schools were educating 76 per cent of the nation's children at elementary level.[21] By this time, however, the amateur parson was having to yield more and more to the trained schoolmaster. Clergy were also public health officers. George Herbert advised clergy to 'mix a little physic', and most clergy acquired some rudimentary medical knowledge.

Each of these duties was looked upon as an aspect of the priest's pastoral concern. Priests felt socially useful and valued members of society. But there were times as a consequence when the national Church seemed to think of itself more like a department of state than a divine society founded by Jesus Christ (a tendency known as erastianism). It was the apparent acceptance of this position by both Church and state that led to the catholic revival in the Church of England in the nineteenth century. In addition, by making every Englishman a member of the Church of England by Act of Parliament and the accident of birth, the evangelistic impulse was anaesthetized. For a large part of Anglican history evangelism seemed almost vulgar since it was unnecessary. As a result, some of those Anglicans who did see the need for it – such as the followers of John Wesley in the eighteenth century – were unable to be contained within the national Church – one of many self-inflicted wounds that the Church was to sustain. Despite the loss of the Methodists, the Church continued to assume that its privileged position in English life would simply carry on with no great evangelistic effort being required. This left it cruelly unprepared for the more secular and plural world that Britain was becoming and that became increasingly hard to ignore from the middle of the nineteenth century.

The 1851 Religious Census, with its revelation that less than half the population was churchgoing, gave the Church of England the shock it needed to further reform and improve its practice. New churches were built in the towns (without which parochial ministry would have been an impossibility). Theological colleges were established and ordination training undertaken more systematically.[22] Above all, it pointed to the need for clergy to be resident if the ideal of Anglican ministry as defined by the Prayer Book and drawn out by George Herbert was to be a reality.

The establishment of the Church of England meant that its prophetic voice was often muted and occasionally fell silent altogether. George Herbert had cautioned those clergy who acted as chaplains to the nobility not to be 'over submissive' but to 'preserve a boldness with them and all, even so far as reproof to their very face, when occasion calls' – though they were to do it 'seasonably and discreetly'.[23] In theory, establishment meant that the Church was in critical solidarity with the state: solidarity, because part of its role was to bless aspects of national and local community life – crowning the sovereign, providing chaplains to the armed forces, marrying and burying parishioners and so on; critical, because the Church would seek to bring to bear through its leaders the Christian gospel at particular moments of national life. This demanded of church leaders not only the courage of their convictions but also a degree of competence in areas for which many of them had little training or first-hand knowledge or experience. The record has been very mixed. The presence of bishops in Parliament led to a disastrous association in the minds of English people between the clergy and the ruling class in the eighteenth century – an association that has long continued – and more specifically between the Church and the Tory Party since the Victorian period. In the late twentieth century, the situation began to change. We can contrast the unwillingness of the bishops – with the notable exception of Bishop Bell of Chichester – to speak out against the policy of obliteration bombing at the end of the Second World War, with the more courageous endorsement by the Archbishop of Canterbury of a damning report – *Faith in the City* – on the plight of the poor in urban priority areas in the 1980s, during Margaret Thatcher's premiership.[24] Part of the problem until relatively recently was that the bishops were drawn from the same leading families that supplied the politicians and generals.[25] However, the numerical weakness of the Church now means that its voice can be more easily dismissed. Although Archbishop Rowan Williams, for example, was clearly ill at ease as the government appeared to be heading towards war with Iraq in 2004, there is little evidence that his views had any influence on national leaders.

The whole notion of an established Church has suffered since the middle years of the nineteenth century from major cultural change: Britain has become an increasingly plural society. The 1851 Census revealed for the first time that there were almost as many Free Church worshippers as Anglicans. This had the effect in the Victorian period of speeding the process of ending Anglican privileges and discrimination against adherents of other Christian denominations. In the present century, with the growth of other religions and the sharp decline of attendance at Christian places of worship, it has made the established position of the Church harder to defend. Yet, paradoxically, this very situation makes some think establishment worth defending. If there are occasions when local communities or the nation as a whole needs to articulate, celebrate or commemorate something collectively, such as the end of a war or the death of a Princess, could a better alternative be found than the rituals of the established Church? The question expects the answer 'No', but a government committed to the modernization of the institutions of the state might well see things differently. Apart from the accident of history, there seems no good reason why a constitutional monarch should be crowned in the cathedral of one Christian denomination, even if other denominations have their representatives present. An entirely civil ceremony in Westminster could easily be devised. There is also no good reason why the leading clergy of one denomination should have their representatives in the Palace of Westminster, and that would apply to other religious groups too. Why should any interest group have a privileged position in a modern British Parliament?

The loss of social value

By the time we come to the twentieth century, we see the Prayer Book's ideal of parochial ministry as Herbert understood it being realized in town and country alike. Anglican clergy were resident in their parishes, better trained than ever before – especially after 1917, when residential training at theological college became a requirement – and committed to the pastoral ideal of Anglican ministry. Parish churches, particularly in the industrial towns, became a hive of activity. Societies and clubs proliferated and often achieved very substantial membership figures. The Sunday School movement was at its height, with over six million children enrolled in 1911.[26] Parishes undertook a range of charitable works and clergy visited their parishioners, exactly as Herbert had commended. Visiting in fact became the chief preoccupation of clergy for large parts of the day, and handbooks commended various ways of visiting methodically and keeping appropriate records. One of my fellow curates in the 1960s was given a visiting list each Monday morning and had to give an account of his endeavours at the staff meeting the following week.

But the situation changed rapidly in three main respects. First, the emerging welfare state began to strip away from the clergy their remaining pastoral functions in the wider community. The professional social worker made the clergyman look amateurish and pastorally redundant. But in the second place, a more secular society, increasingly non-churchgoing, called into question the religious function of the priest as well. Clergy began to look like something from a bygone age. It was hardly surprising, therefore, that the clergy began to feel socially useless and not valued.

But more significant perhaps than either of these factors – though their impact on the clergy can scarcely be exaggerated – was the slowness of the Church in responding to the fast-moving changes of twentieth-century life and culture. Churches are generally a force for conservatism in society: they look back to the past, they stress the value of tradition and continuity, they have long perspectives and tend to eschew violent or sudden change. There are times when such conservatism serves a people well. The recent history of the former eastern bloc countries has shown how the churches can be a source of alternative values, thus keeping alive hope by suggesting that things can be different. But if churches have nothing to contribute towards the issues that most concern contemporary men and women other than hostility or indifference, their influence will correspondingly be diminished. In the nineteenth and early twentieth centuries, all the churches at first resisted almost every aspect of the modern world. They resisted democracy. They resisted Darwinian science. They resisted critical scholarship. They resisted women's emancipation. The Roman Catholic Church did this in characteristically comprehensive fashion when Pius IX issued in 1864 his *Syllabus of Errors*, in which 80 'errors' of the modern period were listed and condemned.[27] But most of the churches shared similar attitudes, and they did this at a time when lay members were becoming educated to higher and higher standards and when the forces of democracy and emancipation in the secular sphere were triumphing. It was almost as if the Church, sensing that it would no longer be the dominant player in the shaping of culture, preferred instead to be in permanent opposition to it rather than have to wrestle with contemporary issues in company with others whose presuppositions it did not share. It was a disastrous mindset. It said, 'We have nothing to say.' And people took note.

The clergy and the liturgy

As the clergy began to lose the dominant roles they once played in society, they turned their attention to those functions that remained to them, especially to their part as leaders of worship and experts in liturgy. From the 1960s, as evidence began to accumulate of the Church's numerical decline, clergy became convinced that a principal reason for the outflow of worshippers was what had once been called the incomparable language of the Book of Common Prayer and the Authorized Version of the Bible. These were now seen as stumbling blocks to the modern generation. (Similar concerns about liturgy were surfacing in other denominations, most notably the Roman Catholic Church and its use of Latin.) The Church that had once created these texts – the Prayer Book and the King James Bible – and in so doing influenced in the most profound way the one language that is spoken across the world, now set about repudiating both in its worship. A period of extensive liturgical experiment and then change followed.

Arguments for liturgical change took various forms. There was, for example, the idea – curiously shared by some evangelicals and some radicals – that the demarcation of sacred and profane should be broken down. Sacred and set-apart buildings and sacred and set-apart guardians of those buildings could only alienate contemporary people. The more churches looked like churches – it was said – the more offputting they became. The more clergy emphasized their calling through the wearing of special clothes – the collar in the street, vestments in the service – the less approachable they seemed. The more the language of worship varied from the language of everyday use, the more it failed to connect with people's mundane lives. Arguments of this kind gathered pace in the latter half of the twentieth century. The result was that some radical clergy abandoned church buildings and traditional liturgy altogether, repudiating what they saw as a fatal theological dualism, opposing sacred and secular, when what was needed was the ability to see the sacred in the secular. Some evangelicals stopped wearing distinctive dress, first as they went about the parish, then when they took part in worship. This had some bizarre results. In one of my neighbouring parishes, for example, the clergy and worship leaders have discarded one set of vestments – cassocks and surplices – for another: red T-shirts bearing the name of the church. The net result of all this was the gradual abandonment not only of the Prayer Book but of many of the assumptions about the role of the Church and the ordained ministry embedded in it.

The clergy – and it was principally a clerical movement – began the work of liturgical renewal and revision. It has had mixed results, though most have been positive and welcomed. The new liturgies, for example, undoubtedly made the services more accessible to most worshippers. Modern translations of the Bible were used and the older language of the liturgy gave way to more contemporary speech. The Eucharist in particular has become more a celebration of all those gathered for worship than something the clergy did on behalf of a largely passive congregation. Almost all the changes have reinforced this sense of greater inclusion: the priest facing the congregation; the greater use of responsive prayer; lay people reading the lessons and leading intercessions; the sharing of the Peace. In addition, liturgical changes saw the role of women enhanced as almost all ministries were opened to them – as readers, servers, intercessors, preachers. At the same time, with the ordination of women to the priesthood the presence of women in the sanctuary in every capacity became commonplace. Worship also became more lively and varied. The new eucharistic liturgies allowed for greater seasonal variation. New collections of hymns appeared, incorporating both older forms of hymn-singing and newer forms of spiritual song. There also developed what has been called 'liturgical ecumenism' as the churches began to co-operate in the production of common eucharistic (and other) texts.[28]

But some people found both the process of change and some of the changes themselves deeply disturbing. The familiar language of services and Scripture ceased to be available, including the traditional form of the Lord's Prayer. For many people this was their most important spiritual resource, to be said whenever they needed to be strengthened and to find God. It was a prayer that united observant Christians and those more distanced from regular worship. In all previous periods clergy knew that if they began, 'Our Father, which art in heaven . . .', in any context, everyone would be able to participate in the prayer from memory. But once the Church began to depart from the traditional words, it caused dismay and confusion. New versions existed in a variety of forms. The most serious result was that the Lord's Prayer ceased to be taught in schools altogether, so that more recent generations have begun their adult lives unable to recite any Christian prayer from memory. This has been a serious, spiritual loss for the British people.

Similarly, the deposition of the Prayer Book has gradually resulted in a multiplicity of services – variety, it was said, is the spice of liturgical life – and the disappearance of 'common' prayer. The Church of England was once united by its liturgy; now it is not only internally divided – people are no longer shaped by a shared liturgy – but those who were only occasional visitors and unable to keep pace with changes were progressively alienated; no one knew any more what to expect when visiting another church.

Many foolish notions lay behind these changes, not all of which came from Christianity. A more emotional culture told clergy that sincerity was unrehearsed and spontaneous. This made clergy deeply suspicious of set liturgies and caused many to privilege the extempore and impromptu. A more entrepreneurial and egalitarian society, where both parents went to work, felt progressively more guilty about its treatment of children. The clerical response was to privilege the 'child-friendly' family service over sung matins or Holy Communion. Changes in secular education were especially influential. Schools gave up rote learning – it was thought to be damaging, stifling spontaneity and suppressing original thinking. Clergy likewise thought there was little merit in the constant repetition and memorizing of liturgies. This was not edifying. It encouraged spiritual lethargy. So seasonal and other variations, and a multiplicity of services of the word, proliferated. It was also said by educationalists that learning came through doing and participating, not hearing and receiving; through activity not passivity. Congregations were made to get up, walk about and offer the Peace to those around them and not merely hear the words during the Eucharist. They were also required to respond more with prayers that included versicles and responses that became ever more didactic and challenging.

Many of the assumptions that lay behind these and other changes were either false or badly applied. Memorizing is an essential part of learning. We need to be able to call upon the spiritual resources of liturgical prayers and biblical passages at points in our lives when we are away from the church context or when Bible and Prayer Book are not to hand. We need the familiarization with texts that repetition makes possible if we are to reflect on them. We need to make beautiful, inspiring, encouraging, disturbing words our own if they are to be an ongoing spiritual resource. The clergy failed to understand that being able to be nourished by texts requires that people 'hear, read, mark, learn and inwardly digest' them – in that order.[29]

The loss of the Prayer Book also meant the loss of the idea of the inclusive Church and the ordained ministry as a kind of national chaplaincy as well. With hindsight we can see that what began as a movement for liturgical renewal ended by having a much wider impact on the spiritual formation of Christian people, sometimes in ways that were not foreseen or intended.

Strengths and weaknesses

The Church of England faces the future, therefore, knowing that it has to work hard to overcome both the climate of indifference and also some aspects of its own legacy. There is a certain apprehension, though one that it shares with all religious bodies. This may be no bad thing if it prompts the Church into a realistic assessment of its strengths and weaknesses. If we review the elements of the classical model of Anglican priesthood, what remains that is of continuing value?

The strengths

The history of the Church of England as established and parochially organized has created a Church that is uniquely situated to play a continuing role in English life. It is ubiquitous: it has sacred buildings, congregations and priests in almost every community. In addition, English men and women on the whole seem to accept that this Church has the right if not the duty to speak for them on particular occasions. These occasions are at many different levels of individual and community life: personal, family, civic and national celebrations and commemorations. The Church of England finds itself in the new millennium 'established' in hearts and minds as much as in law, and this 'establishment' is likely to survive formal disestablishment, at least for a time and perhaps for as long as the Church can remain responsive to people's needs. This could not have been said of the Church in the eighteenth century. Moreover, it is hard to see how any other religious body could now fulfil the same role, or how secular alternatives could easily be provided. It seems unlikely that the nation will want to lose the Church of England even if it has difficulty supporting it by attending on a more regular basis. Having reached this position in English society, however, the clergy need to remind themselves from time to time that this places certain obligations on them. If they fail to meet them, the Church will quickly lose its 'established' status.

The classical model, then, commits Anglicans to the notion of a parish church rather than a congregational or associational church. The parish church has a concern for a defined geographical area and the welfare of everyone within it. The focus of an associational church is the committed membership; the wider community is of concern only as a place of recruitment. This gives a different perspective. It is perfectly true that the advent of the car has made Anglicans much less willing to settle for their parish church if there is another church more to their taste within travelling distance. Nevertheless, even when congregations have large numbers of worshippers who are not of that parish, there is still value in requiring a congregation to earth at least some of its thinking and practical concerns in the geographical parish. It is this that enables Anglican clergy to fulfil what English people expect of them: to be able to articulate on certain specific occasions the core values and beliefs of the English people, and to set the events of every-day life in some wider context of meaning – Wesley Carr's 'interpretive ministry' (see page 63). Those who train ordinands need to help future clergy understand this. Where clergy have never reflected on this aspect of their role or when they incline too far in the direction of an associational understanding of the church, they find these 'community' occasions tedious.

Of course, the reality for many clergy in the contemporary Church, especially in the rural areas, is that they have to operate in several parishes. It is not possible for them to get to know a number of geographical areas as intimately as they once might have got to know one. But clergy are not the only people in the modern world who find themselves living in one place and working in another, or even a number of other places. The type of clergy that will flourish in such situations are those who can build alliances and collaborate with others in ministry. Their local knowledge will be dependent on the quality of partnerships and friendships they make with others.

At the same time, traditional pastoral ministry has to be redefined. Some clergy responded to the advent of the professional social worker and the devaluing of the clerical role by turning priestly ministry into other forms of pastoral work that were valued. Clergy became social workers in the 1960s, political activists in the 1970s, community workers in the 1980s and counsellors in the 1990s. But this was to misunderstand the nature of the clerical pastoral task in modern societies. It had been apparent for some time that the pastoral needs of people in large urban parishes could not be met by one person, however devoted. If needs were to be met, the most significant contribution that the clergy could make was to build up pastorally minded congregations. Lay Christians would be pastors to their neighbours and the congregation a pastoral resource.

But some of the strengths of Anglicanism may be so obvious as to be overlooked. For example, there is every reason to suppose that the demand for the occasional offices, especially baptisms and funerals, will continue as long as the clergy remain sensitive to what people need at these particular moments and are enabled to articulate it in the liturgy.[30] (There is an alarming tendency here for the Liturgical Commission to make new services both wordier and theologically more demanding for the occasional churchgoer.) Similarly there are moments in the life of the nation (Remembrance Day would be a case in point) or in the life of a local community (a tragedy affecting a whole town, such as the murder of a child) where it would be hard to see how a secular ceremony would have the same resonance for people. In addition, we might note the way members of minority faiths value the establishment of the Church of England because it sets religious values at the heart of national life. There is no evidence that other faiths want to see a weakening of the Church's establishment role.

The weaknesses

But there are also weaknesses in the classic model at both national and local level that result from the changes in English society that we noted in Chapter 1. At the beginning of the nineteenth century the Anglican Church dominated the life of English society. Only Anglicans could enter the older universities; only Anglicans could become Members of

Parliament; only Anglicans could be civil servants. The sovereign had to be an Anglican and Anglican bishops sat in the House of Lords. But this was just the tip of the iceberg. At every other level of English society the Anglican Church exercised influence. Over the course of two hundred years all of this was either swept away through legislative change or simply withered away. During the nineteenth century the voice of the Free Churches gathered strength and eventually found political expression through the Liberal Party. The Church of England increasingly identified itself with the Conservative Party, until in the end the Church was described as 'the Tory Party at prayer'. But all this has changed too. The political influence of the Free Churches probably peaked just before the First World War, and it no longer makes any sense at all to speak of the Church of England as the Tory Party at prayer, not least because (as Ted Honderich has pointed out) there simply are not enough Anglicans at prayer to make the claim credible. In other words, the context of Anglican ministry is now so different that if it is to retain its role as chaplain to the nation, it can only do so with the tacit consent of those who are not members. This means, among other things, the stretching of the idea of ecumenism to embrace all the major faiths and not simply other Christian denominations.

But the chief difficulty the Church of England now faces is that of spreading its resources too thinly to be effective at all. It has a glorious inheritance of buildings that at the same time can be a burdensome responsibility. Clergy numbers have fallen to the point where some priests, with or without Reader (lay) ministry, may be trying to maintain services in three, five, ten or more churches each Sunday. This exhausts human and financial resources alike. It also presents a further trap for the unwary.

The Church of England minister performs his or her ministry by being the 'person' in the parish – hence 'parson' – willing to be the focus of certain expectations. Ministers take a lead in encouraging community activities; they support those in need regardless of their religious persuasions or lack of them; they are there to articulate hopes and fears at times of life's transition; the minister becomes a very public person. This is not a ministry where clocking on and off is either appropriate or possible. The danger is that the ordained minister becomes a persona rather than a personality, with the religious role crowding out any other aspect of life. It is worth remembering that the classical Anglican parsons were never wholly consumed by religion and often had other lives – they were farmers or scholars, they had families and kept diaries – without which they would have been impoverished human beings and, as a result, less able to fulfil their ministries. It is not just politicians who need a hinterland.

Conclusion

In surveying the 'classical model', two conclusions now suggest themselves. First, during the twentieth century Britain became less Christian and more diverse: a truly plural society. This fundamentally changes the situation of all the churches, though especially the Church of England as it seeks to be faithful to its mission as the national Church. Establishment is always under scrutiny. It is difficult to argue with the proposition that it is not the business of the liberal state to support or propagate any particular faith but to make it possible for people to hold any belief or none: in that sense, the state is secular. Establishment runs against that principle. Historically it rested on the assumption that the nation was largely (if not exclusively) Christian. Inevitably, therefore, in modern societies, subject to dynamic social and cultural change, the question of establishment can never be a settled one. It may have made sense in Tudor England. It may even have made sense in Victorian England prior to the 1851 Census. But now, with growing numbers of people of other faiths as well as those who are indifferent or hostile to religion, establishment has to be on a different basis if it is to continue. Two possible futures, therefore, present themselves.

On the one hand, it is possible that two large constituencies – religious people who are not Anglican and may not be Christian either, together with that large majority who called themselves 'Christian' in the 2001 Census but are not necessarily churchgoing – may want to retain establishment because they would sooner have religion acknowledged in public life than not. This requires two things of the Church of England. First, it must continue to find creative ways of including not only other Christian groups in national and local celebrations and commemorations, but other faiths, and those with no faith, as occasion demands. It will have to acknowledge the existence of those who have no religious faith. Second, it must also be prepared to go on offering the pastoral offices and seasonal services to people who are not regular attenders. If it retains an appetite to play its traditional role as chaplain to the nation and defender of all faiths, it can have a continuing, albeit reduced, role as the national Church in the foreseeable future. It is even possible that it could do this and survive disestablishment, at least for a time.

On the other hand, it is far from clear that the section of the Church that is growing – the evangelical – is prepared to play such a role with any conviction. For many of them, the chaplaincy role fetters attempts to be truly evangelistic. This attitude has not yet triumphed, but we may be close to a tipping point. If this is the case, then a second future becomes inevitable: the Church will disestablish itself even before

75

legislation to that effect. In fact, a refusal to be the nation's chaplain will make formal disestablishment both necessary and easier to accomplish.

Some Anglicans believe disestablishment will enhance the Church's ability to be prophetic. This is an illusion. The Church may be more free to express its views, but a small, disestablished Church, unwilling to be inclusive, will command less affection and so find it harder to be heard. Paradoxically, disestablishment may mean that the Church is far less influential in the affairs of both the nation and the local community, even if it speaks with less equivocation and a sharper tone about social, economic and political issues. At the moment there is some affection for the Church – an establishment of the heart. It is this affection that leads people to ask for the pastoral offices and look to the parish clergy to manage emotions and point to transcendent meaning at times of community celebration or tragedy. It also enables the clergy to speak out on occasions – as long as that does not become an addiction. But these possibilities will only continue as long as clergy are prepared to be inclusive in their chaplaincy role. How far tomorrow's clergy, drawn increasingly from the growing and more 'exclusivist' congregations, are prepared to adopt and adapt the classical model is probably the key to the Anglican future. It could go either way. We shall have to return to the matter in the final chapter.

4

Evangelical: the minister

That is why there are no hard and fast distinctions between clergy and laymen in the New Testament. All alike are the servants and ministers of God. The New Testament offers us a churchful of ministers!

Michael Green

A man who habitually consults the prophet Isaiah when he is in difficulty is not apt to obey the orders of anyone.

Evelyn Baring, British agent in Egypt, on General Gordon

Origins and evolution

In 1996, the Anglican evangelical church of Holy Trinity, Brompton, put forward plans to create an ecumenical 'millennium village' on a nine-acre site alongside Battersea Power Station in London. Anglican clergy, from the Rural Dean of Battersea to the Archbishop of Canterbury, were grudging in their support. One local priest went so far as to say he was pleased it was to be ecumenical because otherwise he feared the giving of a 'triumphalist Christian message'.[1] The Archbishop said in a sermon at Holy Trinity that it was a 'huge, risk-filled undertaking, and only careful and prayerful consultations will gradually make it clear if it is the will of God'. This was hardly a ringing endorsement. However, one of the Church's leading lay members and its future Supreme Governor, the Prince of Wales, welcomed the idea and wanted to be involved. The plan, as breathtaking as it was costly, and the reactions to it, told us a great deal about the state of the Church of England as the century drew towards its close: only evangelicals had the confidence to dream such dreams and catch the imagination of lay people, and only a tired, uncertain and threatened clergy could give such a cautious response. During the last 30 years of the twentieth century, as the Anglo-Catholic movement withered, evangelicalism enjoyed a revival. It was the only part of the Church of England that showed any signs of numerical growth and, many would argue, the only part that displayed any real life or vigour at all.

Evangelicalism is not confined to the Church of England. Most mainstream Protestant denominations in Britain are either the fruit of the evangelical movement or have been influenced by it. In its more charismatic and Pentecostal forms it has had in recent years considerable evangelistic success across the world, not least in countries that have traditionally been strongholds of Roman Catholicism.[2] But what is distinctive about evangelical Christianity? What makes a Christian an evangelical?

Evangelicalism and the Age of Enlightenment

The term 'evangelical' can be found as early as the sixteenth century: Sir Thomas More calls those who urged the reformation of the Church 'Evaungelicalles'.[3] In doing so he is pointing to that 'religious outlook which makes the primary point of Christian reference the Good News of the *Evangelion*, or the text of the Scripture generally'.[4] But the term was not widely used until the nineteenth century when it came to be applied to certain revivalist clergy of the previous century who called themselves 'church-men' or 'gospel-men'.[5] In other words, while strands within the evangelical tradition can be traced back to the Reformation period, the real origins of evangelical Christianity lie at the beginning of the modern period when claims to knowledge and truth began to be tested by reason and the scientific method. Evangelicalism was both a consequence of these wider cultural movements and a reaction against them. We could say, therefore, that the Age of Reason made both positive and negative contributions to the development of this form of popular Christianity. I say this because there is a tendency on the part of some historians, and some evangelicals themselves, to see evangelicalism simply as a continuation of Reformation Protestantism whose only relationship to the Enlightenment was to repudiate most aspects of it.[6]

Negatively, there were two aspects of the Enlightenment that the evangelicals certainly did reject. In the first place they turned their backs on the bloodless God of the eighteenth-century rationalists and deists – Voltaire's architect of the universe, the great geometrician, who had set the world in motion and given it laws by which to exist, but who now stood apart from it like a master craftsman observing the artefact he had made.[7] For evangelicals, God was above all the God who *intervened* in creation – in miracles, in answers to prayer and supremely in Jesus Christ. For most eighteenth-century Christians, the world was an ordered and predictable place because it operated according to 'laws which never shall be broken';[8] but for the evangelical the world was a place of continuous surprise as God made his power and presence felt in unpredictable ways.[9]

Then in the second place the evangelicals rejected a fundamental tenet of the Enlightenment: the idea that human reason is the only or the only reliable source of knowledge. They were not anti-reason, but they firmly believed that the religious truths that reason discovered – the God of Deism – only took the believer so far: there were also the truths of revelation. In addition, they repudiated the idea that 'enthusiasm' had no place in religion. The previous age, the age of Civil War, had been emotionally highly charged and people had recoiled from its fanaticism; the evangelicals argued, however, that no one could hear the gospel preached and remain unmoved. An emotionless Christianity produced spiritual deadness. They turned away from the version of Christianity that emerged in the Anglican Church under the influence of these assumptions – rational and unemotional. It tended to make God remote and was more interested in morality than doctrine. The sermons of the day were typically concerned with such topics as what made for good manners and polite behaviour.[10] The virtues the preachers encouraged are revealingly displayed on the tombstones of the period: 'Polished Manners, inflexible Integrity, and the warmest Benevolence of Heart'; 'One of the most valuable women that ever liv'd, whose principal Happiness consisted (Altho' she was of some rank) in real and unbounded Affectionn and Tenderness for her husband and children'. Reacting against this, evangelicals believed Christianity had to be first heard as gospel rather than wisdom. Above all, the eighteenth-century evangelicals repudiated the tendency to complacency in religion that an age of optimism about human capacities tended to produce.

But evangelicalism was also a *product* of the Enlightenment, the result of Protestant Christianity adapting itself to a changing cultural idiom. The early evangelicals – such as John Wesley – were learned men, steeped in the new ways of thinking. In key respects they were influenced by Enlightenment assumptions. Far from rejecting reason *tout court*, the evangelicals accepted that it had a role to play in determining truth in religion as in other spheres. Wesley said, 'It is a fundamental principle with us that to renounce reason is to renounce religion, that religion and reason go hand in hand, and that all irrational religion is false religion.'[11] But Christianity was also concerned with that knowledge of God in the Bible which, while not being irrational, could not be obtained by reason but only by God's choosing to reveal himself. What held the two together was the Enlightenment assumption that the basis of all knowledge is *experience*. For evangelicals, real Christianity was 'experimental' (that is, experiential), a religion based on practical experience in the same way that science was based on the inductive method.

In addition, the first evangelicals generally shared the optimism of the age, though fiercely resisting the religious complacency to which it could so easily give rise. The secular viewpoint that human beings were capable of steady improvement was matched by an 'optimism of grace', a theology of God's good providence that said that individual human beings could become, with the Holy Spirit's assistance, what God intended them to be and grace was not restricted to some small band of elect people (as Calvinists taught). This lay behind both the evangelicals' passion for evangelism and their irrepressible joy. Moreover, this gradual change for the better in people consequent upon evangelistic activity and the acceptance of the gospel would finally issue in the return of Christ and the dawn of the age of righteousness. In this respect too evangelicals shared with their contemporaries an optimistic view of the future that became in the wider culture of the nineteenth century a belief in human progress that was only finally shattered on the battlefields of the First World War. But evangelical optimism was balanced by the firm conviction that by themselves human beings could do nothing; they were mired in sin; they could not save themselves; they needed a saviour.

Anglican evangelicals of the eighteenth and nineteenth centuries need to be distinguished from evangelicals in other churches, especially Methodists – though some Methodists were known as 'Church Methodists' until at least the 1830s.[12] While there are many family resemblances, there were some theological and ecclesiological differences. Anglican evangelicals were, for example, more Calvinistic than the Wesleyan Methodists, generally rejecting Wesley's idea that it was possible for people to be made perfect in the love of God and delivered from all sin. They were also content to remain within an episcopally ordered and established Church. Edward Bickersteth, who helped to found the inter-denominational Evangelical Alliance in 1846, regarded anti-establishment sentiment among Dissenters (the Free Churches) as 'poison in the veins of dissent'.[13] In particular, evangelicals valued the Book of Common Prayer. It was doctrinally sound and its prescribed liturgies captured in wonderful language the heart of true worship. Charles Simeon said that no other book outside Holy Scripture was as free from error or as uplifting. Evangelicals were never a majority of the Anglican clergy in the nineteenth century – perhaps a third were by the middle years – but they were influential beyond their numbers. By the end of the twentieth century, only evangelical clergy were likely to witness significant growth in the numbers attending their churches. Despite this, they remain relatively under-represented among the Church of England hierarchy.

Four characteristics of evangelicalism

Although evangelicalism has taken various forms over the centuries and different doctrines have assumed different degrees of prominence at different times, there are common features that enable us to identify a definite tradition of evangelical Christianity. In a comprehensive study of modern evangelicalism, the historian D. W. Bebbington notes four in particular, each of which had implications for ordained ministry.[14]

First, evangelicals make the need for *conversion* central to Christian faith and life. Human beings are fallen creatures who can only be saved if they have faith in Jesus Christ and experience for themselves a 'new birth'. Wesley's account of his own conversion in 1738 is a classic description of the evangelical experience:

> In the evening I went very unwillingly to a society in Aldersgate Street, where one was reading Luther's preface to the Epistle to the Romans. About a quarter to nine, while he was describing the change which God works in the heart through faith in Christ, I felt my heart strangely warmed. I felt I did trust in Christ, Christ alone for salvation; and assurance was given me that he had taken away my sins, even mine, and saved me from the law of sin and death.[15]

In previous centuries there has been as much emphasis on damnation as salvation in evangelical preaching. Victorian sermons were a mix of what Owen Chadwick has called the 'blast of judgement and sweetness of promise'.[16] This may be more muted now, but the contemporary preacher continues to have in mind the need for life-changing decision, for to be a Christian is to have had such an experience and to know for oneself the meaning of the core Protestant doctrine of justification by grace through faith.

Some evangelicals, though by no means all, taught that conversion was at a precise and unforgettable moment of time. Many evangelical hymns reflect this intense emotional experience:

> Long my imprisoned spirit lay
> fast bound in sin and nature's night;
> thine eye diffused a quick'ning ray,
> I woke, the dungeon flamed with light;
> my chains fell off, my heart was free;
> I rose, went forth, and followed thee.[17]

At one time, the obituaries of Methodist ministers recorded not their birth and death but the date of their conversion and their death. People might have been baptized or have been a member of a church for many years or even be ordained, but unless they could point to this conversion experience they had not begun to know what Christianity was about.

Conversion had a corollary and a consequence. The corollary was the idea of assurance. Those who were converted knew that they were saved.

The experience was so overwhelming that there was no room for doubt; the prevailing emotion is always overwhelming gratitude and joy. The consequence was that lives had to change, for how could a person be truly converted if his or her life showed no sign of moral regeneration?

A second characteristic of evangelical Christianity is its *busyness*. Evangelical Christians are committed to a life of ceaseless work in the Lord's vineyard – praying, studying the Scriptures, encouraging fellow Christians and, above all, evangelizing. One nineteenth-century evangelical, Stevenson Blackwood, who said it was better to 'wear out than to rust out', has left an account of a journey he once took by train from Aberdeen to London. He handed out tracts and preached to the fishermen on the quay before the train left, gave a book to a woman in the ticket queue, prayed with a drunk between Aberdeen and Perth, exchanged a tract for a sermon by Spurgeon with a woman at Edinburgh station, woke a snoring man on the journey south and read a tract to him, distributed books to others and spent the final hour writing an address.[18] It is not surprising to discover that in the last century the Wesleyan Methodists had a 'Worn-out ministers' fund'! Contemporary evangelicals will invariably give many evenings and weekends to both overtly Christian and other community activities, the latter providing further evangelistic opportunities.

The compulsion to witness to all and sundry is in some contrast to the catholic tradition. Anglo-Catholics were shocked at the way evangelical preachers put before their audiences some of the deepest mysteries of the Christian religion in their efforts to convert. The catholics taught 'reserve in communicating religious knowledge'.[19] Potential and new Christians needed milk before they could feast on meat. Besides, these were holy and sacred matters and should not be lightly dispensed.

In the third place evangelical Christianity is *Bible-centred* – as the very term evangelical suggests. There are two aspects to this. First, the Bible is regarded as the ultimate authority in matters of doctrine and morality. Earlier generations of evangelicals accepted the Bible as 'the word of God' but did not elaborate any theory of infallibility. But from the 1820s a major strand of evangelical opinion began to insist on the Bible as verbally inspired and literally true. This was in part a reaction against trends within academic theology that increasingly began to study the Bible like all other ancient documents.[20] This is not to say that evangelicals cannot be open to receive new knowledge about the Bible. The expounding and interpretation of God's word is a continuing activity of the Church. The test, however, is always a Christian one: does it tend towards greater edification? In this respect we can see lines of continuity with the reformed tradition of the sixteenth-century reformation, as this statement by the Synod of Berne in 1986 reveals:

But where something is brought before us by our pastors or by others, which brings us closer to Christ, and in accordance with God's word is more conducive to mutual friendship and Christian love than the interpretation now presented, we will gladly accept it and will not limit the course of the Holy Spirit, which does not go backwards towards the flesh but always forward towards the image of Jesus Christ our Lord.[21]

Second, the Bible was revered as a medium of God's continuing presence. Catholic Anglicans drew near to God and felt his presence with them as they knelt before the Blessed Sacrament; evangelical Anglicans as they read his word.

Finally, evangelical Christianity is Christ-centred – or, more particularly, it is *centred on Christ's saving death on the cross*. The cross (often with a capital C) is the theme of many evangelical hymns both old and new, as these verses from a nineteenth-century and a twentieth-century hymn respectively show:

> In the Cross of Christ I glory.
> Towering o'er the wrecks of time,
> All the light of sacred story
> Gathers round its head sublime.[22]

> From heaven You came,
> Helpless babe,
> Entered our world,
> Your glory veiled;
> Not to be served
> But to serve,
> And give Your life
> That we might live.[23]

The cross is always at the heart of evangelical theology and worship because it points to the central evangelical doctrine: the atonement. Christianity is above all a religion of salvation. It offers to sinful human beings the means of escaping from what is otherwise their inevitable destiny, namely eternal perdition. There is nothing people can do to gain salvation for themselves since even their best endeavours are tainted with sin. But God intervened in history in Jesus Christ in order to reconcile people to himself. Jesus lived the perfect life of obedience to the Father and never wavered in that obedience, even on the cross. The cross became the place where atonement was wrought by Jesus Christ. Those who put their trust in him, and not in any works of their own, can find their salvation.

Not the labours of my hands
Can fulfil thy law's demands;
Could my zeal no respite know,
Could my tears for ever flow,
All for sin could not atone:
Thou must save, and Thou alone.

Nothing in my hand I bring,
Simply to Thy Cross I cling;
Naked, come to Thee for dress;
Helpless, look to Thee for grace;
Foul, I to the fountain fly;
Wash me, Saviour, or I die.[24]

But why should the *death* of Christ have brought about atonement? Historically, Christian theology has never definitively resolved the question. There has never been any creedal formula as there has been with the question of the nature of Christ as human and divine, or the relationship between the three Persons of the Trinity. As a result we can discern two principal ways in which Christ's death has been understood by the Church.

In one, Christ is thought of as a *representative* of the human race. From birth to death he lives a life as God would have it – in complete obedience to the will of God – and so without sin. The emphasis is on the life lived, for it is this that God wants, not death. But this obedient life leads to his rejection by his contemporaries: his gracious words and wonderful deeds – the demonstration of the love and generosity of God – provoke rage and spite and lead to his death on the cross. His career becomes not only the perfect life offered to God but also a bloody sacrifice. Salvation for all others comes through being able to identify themselves with Christ by having faith in him. They thereby make their own this perfect offering – a life that is obedient even to death on the cross – simply by clinging to his cross. This in turn produces in the believer change in behaviour and attitude.

The second interpretation, generally favoured by evangelicals, sees greater significance in the actual death: Christ dies not as a representative but as a *substitute* for sinful humanity. Human beings deserve the punishment of death and damnation for their sins, for as St Paul wrote, the wages of sin is death. But Christ took the punishment of all others on himself by substituting himself for us and dying in our place – a sacrificial death. However, because he was sinless, God raised Jesus from death and restored him to life, eternal life. Those who put their trust in Christ are enabled to participate in this life. It is this doctrine that lies behind not only the experience of conversion but also the subsequent life of the Christian, for the Christian life is essentially one of gratitude for what Christ has done for us on the cross.

I am not sure how great the distinction between Christ as representative and Christ as substitute really is, since both ways of looking at Christ's death have elements of representation and substitution. But the idea of 'penal substitution' is very hard for many non-evangelicals to accept. For them the idea of God punishing the innocent on behalf of the guilty, however willingly the innocent accepts the penalty, is simply immoral.

But the doctrine of the cross produced controversy among evangelicals themselves. They divided over the question, 'For whom did Christ die?' Some evangelicals, influenced by Calvin's doctrine of predestination, assert that Christ died only for those whom God had already determined should inherit eternity; others, Arminians, believed that Christ died for all and so all could be saved if they called on him. This issue divided most Methodist (Arminian) from Anglican (Calvinistic) evangelicals until the nineteenth century. Since then the difference between the two has largely been one of emphasis: some evangelicals emphasize the grace of God (a more Calvinistic emphasis), others the need for human repentance (Arminian), in the Christian life. During the 1870s, the American evangelist Dwight L. Moody, who leaned towards Arminianism, had a successful evangelistic ministry in Britain, preaching the grace of God available to all and calling on individuals to make a decision for Christ – which further diminished more Calvinistic evangelicalism. His influence continues through the hymns to which he and Ira Sankey introduced his British audiences.

The model

How, then, did this theology affect the theory and practice of ordained ministry? When we turn to consider the evangelical understanding of ordained ministry, three theological ideas are of central importance in determining how that is to be understood: the priesthood of all believers; personal salvation; the Bible as the word of God.

The priesthood of all believers

Although the word 'priest' occurs in the Book of Common Prayer, evangelicals are generally wary of using it, preferring to call clergy 'ministers'. There are two reasons for this. The first has to do with the word 'priest' and the other with the word 'minister'.

The underlying reason for evangelical unease with the word priest has its roots in the New Testament, where it is only ever used of the Jewish priesthood and Jesus, our great High Priest. The leaders of the

Christian community are never called priests. The function of the priest in the Jerusalem Temple at the time of Jesus was to act as intermediary between God and people. On behalf of the worshipper, the priest would offer animal sacrifice as an expression of the worshipper's desire to renew or restore his relationship with God. The worshipper associated his life with that of the animal, whose life was then given back to God through the shedding of blood. Priests acted on behalf of and in the place of lay people, doing for them what they could not do for themselves. Of especial importance was the role of the High Priest on the annual Day of Atonement. On that day, the High Priest passed through the curtain or veil that separated the innermost part of the Temple from the rest of the building, entered the holy of holies that lay beyond it, and through the symbolic slaughter of an unblemished animal secured the reconciliation of the whole of Israel with God. But these animal sacrifices had to be endlessly repeated. When Christians reflected on the death of Christ and tried to make sense of it, they did so in the light of these Temple offerings. Christ's death on the cross was understood as a sacrificial death, indeed, the only truly efficacious sacrifice, because, unlike the Temple offerings, it only needed to be made once-for-all, rendering superfluous the repeated animal sacrifices in the Temple, and so the order of priests. Moreover, it was made for the whole of humanity and not just Jews. In the crucifixion of Christ, God and humanity were reconciled – Jesus is both true High Priest and effective victim – which was why, according to the evangelists, the veil of the Temple, which had separated people from the holy of holies, was torn in two (Mark 15.38): Christ had opened the way for all human beings to enter the holy of holies.

Evangelicals, therefore, take the general Protestant position that in so far as the word priest suggests an intermediary between God and humanity, it has no scriptural warrant. There is only one intermediary and that is Jesus, our great High Priest. The term priest is, therefore, best avoided – even if it is in the Prayer Book – because it may mislead. (We might note, however, that many contemporary evangelicals – unlike their forebears – will have little or no experience of using the Prayer Book or knowledge of its contents.) The New Testament does, however, speak of the Christian community as a whole as a royal priesthood:

> But you are a chosen race, a royal priesthood, a holy nation, God's own people, that you may declare the wonderful deeds of him who called you out of darkness into his marvellous light . . . (1 Peter 2.9, RSV)

If there is only one true priest – Christ – how or in what sense can the Church be a priesthood? St Paul gives the answer in a striking phrase:

the Church is the Body of Christ. The risen and ascended Christ – he who is our great High Priest – chooses to be present now in his Church: it is his body. To encounter the Church is to encounter Christ – as Paul discovered on the Damascus road (Acts 9.5). This is not to say that the Church *is* Christ, for then we would worship the Church and not Christ – an idolatrous identification that some Christians have sometimes made. The Church expresses Christ, makes him real and visible, 'demonstrates Him without being confounded with Him'.[25] The Church is a royal priesthood as it opens itself up to the Holy Spirit and lives out the priestly way of life of Jesus Christ, especially as Jesus commanded in the context of his passion. At the Last Supper, when Jesus washed his disciples' feet, he gave his Church a pattern of priestly service that they were to imitate. The Church is a royal priesthood when it washes feet.

There can be no suggestion that this priestly ministry is confined to the ordained. It is the business of the whole Church. This is the starting point for any understanding of ordained ministry and we can begin to see why evangelicals are unhappy with the word priest when applied to clergy. Their preference is for 'minister' – the Latin word for servant. But the clergy are not the only ministers. The Church as a whole is a minister (servant) to the world. Each Christian is a minister to his fellow Christians and to his neighbour. The *ordained* ministers are simply those who have a particular function within the servant Church. Before we consider what that function is, a further word needs to be said about the context in which the ordained ministers minister.

Personal salvation

The heart of evangelicalism is personal experience of Jesus Christ as the one who saves. Those who are able to say not just 'Jesus is Lord' but 'Jesus is *my* Lord' as a result of such experience are those called out by God from among the generality of humanity to be his Church. To them God gives gifts of the Spirit. Several things follow from this that help to shape the evangelical understanding of what it is to be an ordained minister.

First, this understanding of Christianity is radically egalitarian. It is *egalitarian* because it places the emphasis not on any hierarchy of ordained people (the tendency of catholicism) but on the whole people of God. The New Testament word for church – *ecclesia* – refers to all those who have named the name of Jesus Christ and walk within the company of Christians. It is *radically* egalitarian because God may call and convert and equip for ministry anyone regardless of status, rank, age, gender or qualification, including moral qualification. (Understanding this was one of the great contributions to Christianity of St Paul. Recovering it was one of the great contributions of Martin Luther.) What is important is not whether you are ordained or lay, or whether you have been a member of the Church over many years or only a short while, or whether you have received much or little formal education, or whether you are morally worthy, but whether you are converted and baptized or not. The only distinction between people that counts is the distinction between converted and unconverted. Once you are within the community of the faithful, distinctions are few and relate to charismatic gifts. This creates a church ethos that is quite different from that of the catholic movement. Evangelicalism is essentially a movement of the man or woman in the pew, the ordinary Christian; Anglo-Catholicism, by contrast, is clerical and hierarchical. Evangelicals experience the Church not so much as a divinely founded institution, stretching back through the centuries to the time of the apostles, as a living fellowship of like-minded believers stretching throughout the contemporary world. Anglo-Catholics are always looking back, Evangelicals are always looking around.

Evangelicalism is also non-hierarchical and democratic in that the gifts of the Spirit are distributed by God without regard to human distinctions. The gifts of healing, preaching or teaching, for example, are not confined to ordained pastors. God calls whomsoever he will to exercise these different ministries within congregations. In Anglo-Catholic circles, priests are generally deferred to. Evangelicals have to be ready for the Spirit to make himself known through anyone, whether ordained or lay. (However, 'discerning the spirits', helping people to distinguish true manifestations of the Spirit from the false and misleading, is an important part of ordained ministry – though not ordained ministry alone.)

The Bible as the word of God

For evangelicals, as we have seen, the Bible plays a central role. If the spirituality of catholics can be described as 'sacramental', that of evangelicals can be called 'biblical'. This is not to deny that catholics read the Bible or evangelicals receive the sacrament. But it is to draw attention to the fact that the evangelical approaches the word of God as contained in Holy Scripture with the same reverence and expectation as the catholic approaches the altar. Here is the place where Jesus Christ is to be encountered – in the reading and the preaching of the word. Moreover, evangelicals formed in the Anglican tradition of morning and evening prayer (matins and evensong) recognize that before the word can be preached it must be heard – and that means it must be read. The regular reading of the Old and New Testaments is an essential ingredient of evangelical spirituality, as it is of Cranmer's Book of Common Prayer. There is no requirement in Cranmer's service of matins for the preaching of a sermon. The worshipper would encounter God directly through hearing his word. As Martin Luther expressed it, the New Testament is the manger where Christ is laid.

The particular role of the ordained

All of this creates quite a different ethos in which the work of the ordained is to be understood. In the catholic revival in the Church of England the role of the ordained was pivotal. Anglo-Catholicism was clerical and churchy – it was about priests and sacraments and ritual. The focus was decidedly in the chancel. The tendency of catholicism is to think in ontological and hierarchical terms. Being a priest is not a matter of function, or not only a matter of function; it is first and foremost a matter of 'being'. A person is 'formed' as a priest. There is an ontological change such that 'once a priest always a priest'. Moreover, the clergy are in the top part of the institutional pyramid with the bishops at the apex. There is a top-down attitude and approach: authority and power come down from above. Catholic clergy tend to see lay involvement in church affairs in terms of the clergy giving to the laity a share of their power.

The evangelical tradition has a quite different orientation. Ordained ministry is seen in more functional terms. The clergy are the servants or ministers of the congregation. The focus is hardly ever on the Church as an institution, hardly ever building-centred: it is on the congregation(s). Evangelicals see this reflected in Article XIX of the Thirty-Nine Articles of Religion, where the ordained ministry is put in its proper place as servants of that congregation, stewards of the word and sacrament:

> The visible Church of Christ is a congregation of faithful men, in the which the pure Word of God is preached, and the Sacraments be duly ministered according to Christ's ordinance in all those things that of necessity are requisite to the same.[26]

The visible Church is the Body of Christ on earth but it exists in that time between the exaltation of Christ after his resurrection (the ascension) and his final coming again (the *parousia*). It consists of those who have responded to the gospel and been baptized – the congregation of faithful men and women. But it is not a perfect society. It needs all the time to be renewed and purified by word and sacrament and the responsibility for ensuring that this happens lies with the ordained ministers.

The ordained minister, therefore, is first of all a preacher and expounder of God's word. Since salvation depends upon responding to the gospel message, that message must be preached. Preaching for conversions will always be an aspect of evangelical preaching not only because people who have never heard the gospel may attend a service but also because even long-standing members of congregations may not in fact be converted. One nineteenth-century vicar in Cornwall, William Haslam, reported that he was converted by his own preaching! As a result, evangelical ministers will spend a good deal of time studying the Scriptures and preparing themselves for teaching occasions and for preaching. In contemporary evangelical churches the sermon will still occupy a substantial amount of time – 20 to 40 minutes would not be unusual – and pulpits, even in Anglican churches, still have a commanding if not central place. Sermons are taken seriously – and serious means long! At any rate, evangelical sermons will be more than the rather perfunctory eight minutes of other Anglicans. While recognizing that lay Christians may equally have a gift of preaching, study of the Scriptures and the careful preparation of sermons is one of the most important duties of evangelical clergy. In this, evangelicals take to heart the question of the Bishop in the Ordinal to those about to be ordained as priest:

> Will you be diligent in Prayers, and in reading of the holy Scriptures, and in such studies as help to the knowledge of the same, laying aside the study of the world and the flesh?[27]

Then second, the ordained minister ensures that the sacraments are celebrated. The sacraments, in line with the Articles, are those 'ordained of Christ' – the two gospel sacraments of baptism and the Holy Communion:

> Those five commonly called Sacraments, that is to say, Confirmation, Penance, Orders, Matrimony, and Extreme Unction, are not to be counted for Sacraments of the Gospel ... for that they have not any visible sign of ceremony ordained of God.[28]

In the third place, because the priesthood of all believers is emphasized, an important function of ordained ministry is the discernment and development of the Spirit-given (charismatic) gifts of others so that they too may exercise some ministry of service. This also means creating congregations in which there is an expectation that gifts are given to all and will be discerned among the laity.

The model in practice

In the contemporary Church there are two types of evangelical congregation: the charismatic and the non-charismatic. Both share the same commitment to the Scriptures, but the charismatic congregations are marked by more lively and exuberant worship and set great store by certain manifestations of the Spirit.

Charismatic congregations first appeared in the UK during the 1960s. Many evangelicals, though by no means all, in almost all Protestant denominations began to experience charismatic renewal – an intense experience of the Holy Spirit. (There was a parallel movement within Roman Catholicism after 1967, and clear affinities with Pentecostalism.[29]) The first Anglican parish to be affected collectively was St Mark's, Gillingham. This experience was something over and above initial conversion and was understood as a deep renewal of Christian life through a release of the Holy Spirit that had been given in baptism, or a fresh outpouring of, or baptism in, the Holy Spirit. It resulted in more joyous worship (sometimes expressed bodily with applause, arm-raising and calling out – hence the pejorative term 'happy clappies') and a new appreciation of those charismatic gifts of the Spirit mentioned in the New Testament – such as speaking in tongues. Sometimes it was accompanied by 'signs and wonders' – miraculous healings, dramatic occurrences (such as the Toronto blessing) and radically changed lives (drug addicts or criminals who turned away from their past). In each case, groups of Christians, or whole congregations, were given new fervour in worship and witness alike. The collective term for all this was 'renewal'. Some have described these kinds of experiences as a second Pentecost. A recent Archbishop of Canterbury, George Carey, has described how while on a visit to Canada he had such an experience of renewal that his life was quite transformed:

It restored me to a great love of Christ, a deep desire to read the Scriptures, a longing to share the Christian faith with others and a desire to praise God.[30]

These charismatic manifestations restored to Christians, battered by the cold winds of secularism, something that the early Church knew well: the idea of *dunamis* – power. The capacity to turn lives round was real power. It is these demonstrations that have enabled charismatic forms of evangelicalism and Pentecostalism to make converts in great numbers across many parts of the contemporary world. It has truly empowered the poor.

But as well as these experiences being innately satisfying, they also become important tests of discipleship. The prevailing culture sets a high premium on feelings as a mark of sincerity and authenticity; charismatic evangelicals are, in this respect, deeply influenced by contemporary culture. For them, emotion also becomes a test for reality, sincerity and truth – in religion.[31] As a result, when individuals or groups have not seen their particular charismatic experiences replicated in the congregation more generally, they are tempted to judge and find wanting their fellow Christians, sometimes leaving the Anglican Church for more explicitly charismatic ones.

But some evangelicals have been wary of charismatic congregations, fearing that an undue emphasis on charismatic gifts can lead to the setting aside of the wisdom and discipline of duly appointed leaders, or to individual leaders convincing themselves that everything they do is under the immediate direction of the Holy Spirit and so exempt from any human scrutiny or judgement. This is no theoretical or hypothetical risk. In Sheffield in the 1980s there was just such an occurrence. Some members of the evangelical congregation at St Thomas Crookes were deeply affected by a visiting American preacher, John Wimber, and a Signs and Wonders Conference he held in the city in 1985. After the conference, they began to hold alternative services for younger adults at nine o'clock on Sunday evenings. There was a great deal of experimentation in music, the use of projected images and special lighting effects. Numbers multiplied, the Nine O'Clock Service (NOS), as it became known, outgrew St Thomas and relocated in the Ponds Forge building in the town centre. A leader, Chris Brain, emerged and was fast-tracked to ordination by the diocese.[32] Under his direction new theological themes were pursued: a mix of New Age and the Creation spirituality of the former American Dominican monk, Matthew Fox.[33] Fox taught that Christians should make the centre of their spiritual life the idea of the goodness of creation rather than the traditional evangelical starting point of a fallen world and original sin. This was given liturgical expression in what Brain called the Planetary Mass. Sin, according to Brain, was not a consequence of disobeying God but of being disconnected from his creation. It is hard to think of anything further away from conservative evangelical theology. Clergy in nearby parishes began to hear disturbing stories about what was taking place at the NOS. The diocesan hierarchy, pleased at being able to point to an example of spectacular growth, especially among young people – numbers reached about 600 – continued to give NOS their blessing and refused to listen to those who were growing alarmed. Eventually, ten years after NOS started, it became clear that something not unlike a cult had developed and there were accusations of bullying and sexual harassment. The whole experiment was brought to an end in 1995 – though not before some lives had been damaged. Most of the young people left in disillusion.

The non-charismatic evangelical churches would see in the St Thomas experiment a paradigm case of a congregation that does not allow its charismatic experience to be scrutinized by the wider Christian community – in this case the normal Anglican structures of deanery and diocese.[34] There is no testing of the spirits.[35] For conservative evangelicals, there can be no shortcut to truth or salvation by way of mystical experience, and much danger in heading down that pathway. A faithful congregation is one where the Bible is taught and minister and congregation sit patiently week by week under God's word.

Strengths and weaknesses

The strengths

Evangelicals sometimes claim that they are 'counter-cultural'. In so far as the culture is secular this may be true. Yet in many respects the evangelical model of ministry is particularly well suited to these times. The twentieth century saw the triumph of the market economy and the democratic polity. In other words, ordinary people became used to having a large measure of control over their own lives, exercising choices in both the market place and politics, and being less deferential. In addition, we saw the rise of a more emotional culture. The evangelical form of Christianity – especially the more charismatic – fits this situation well. On the one hand, while retaining such traditional doctrines as the utter sinfulness of humanity over against the holiness of God, it actually believes in and exemplifies the possibility of radical change in human lives: the Holy Spirit transforms lives, enabling ordinary people to realize God-given potential. On the other hand, although some evangelical churches can be quite authoritarian, Anglican evangelicalism in the main invites people to join a local congregation in which differences between clergy and laity are not greatly emphasized and leadership – which is to be exercised collaboratively – is understood in terms of loving service. Charismatic evangelicals are undoubtedly more comfortable with a less hierarchical Church in which the ordinary lay worshipper is genuinely encouraged and empowered. This often makes them indifferent and sometimes hostile towards the institutional hierarchy of the Church of England – and is one reason why evangelicals are disproportionately fewer in senior posts: they are not that bothered about jobs that are often little more than administrative and managerial. In this respect, the evangelical argues that this practice of the Church is more faithful to the gospel injunction of Jesus that within the community of those who would be his disciples there must be no lording it over one another:

> You know that the rulers of the Gentiles lord it over them, and their great ones are tyrants over them. It will not be so among you; but whoever wishes to be great among you must be your servant, and whoever wishes to be first among you must be your slave; just as the Son of Man came not to be served but to serve, and to give his life a ransom for many.[36]

The lay Christian is undoubtedly empowered in the evangelical congregation in a way that is less true in many middle-of-the-road Anglican
parishes and almost impossible among Anglo-Catholics. Many lay people
have discovered a vocation as a worship leader (a position that often
rivals that of the ordained minister in importance) or preacher or
teacher or evangelist. While ordination may be necessary to preside at
the Eucharist it is certainly not sufficient to carry authority within the
evangelical community. If ordained ministers are to have authority it
must also be because they serve the congregation and because they are
able to testify in their own lives to the transforming work of the
Spirit. (Article XXVI of the Thirty-Nine Articles, which speaks of the
unworthiness of the minister as not hindering the efficacy of word and
sacrament, may be acknowledged in theory, but in practice ministers
who could not speak from a continuing personal experience of God's
power at work in them would soon find their authority to preach and
preside undermined: personal experience rather than ordination is in the
end the decisive factor.)

The more democratic spirit of the evangelical congregations sets a
high premium, therefore, on clergy being warm and approachable and
willing to share ministry with others. There is no room here for the
socially superior parson or the non-collaborator or the rather reserved,
slightly aloof, somewhat bookish, often eccentric, saintly priest of the
Anglo-Catholic tradition. One of the strengths of the evangelical clergy is
that they could easily be your next-door neighbour. If they exemplify
holiness, it is the kind of holiness that anyone could aspire to.

A final strength of evangelicalism is its gift for popular music.
Methodism, it has often been said, was born in song. In fact, most forms
of evangelical Christianity have set great store by singing – from the
simple chorus of the beach mission to the rich musicality and theology
of the great evangelical hymn-writers. It was not only William Booth
who took the view that the devil should not have all the best tunes; the
Methodists raided any secular source, however profane, if it yielded sing-
able music. John and Charles Wesley recognized the power of music in
moving hearts, and borrowed from many places, including other religious
traditions. The value of songs for teaching had been understood from
the earliest days of Christianity. The early fourth-century heretic, Arius,
had used music to propagate his doctrines; it was said that the dockers
in the port of Alexandria sang Arian hymns as they went about their
work. Evangelical worship serves to remind other Christians that the
faith may be more easily and effectively communicated sung than said.
However, the more recent and more charismatic evangelical churches
have tended to regard the function of music in worship as emotional
rather than didactic. They are less concerned with the presentation in

an accessible form of doctrine than with enabling the expression of feeling about or towards God. The contemporary spiritual song stirs the soul, removes inhibition and moves the worshipper closer to God.

The weaknesses

Some of the greatest strengths of the evangelical model are also its greatest weaknesses. For instance, evangelicalism places considerable emphasis on the experience of being saved (conversion), leading to changed lives and personal holiness. But this can present problems for clergy. Emphasis on what we might call the visible evidence of salvation – changed lives of a particular quality – places a considerable burden of expectation on ordained ministers. Evangelical clergy are required by their congregations to be exemplars of the Christian life. They are, therefore, likely to be more severely judged in such matters as sexual orientation or marital failure than clergy in other traditions. When clergy fall from grace, the pain of letting down a congregation – which is a factor for clergy in any tradition – is likely to be especially painful and disorientating for evangelicals. In 1999, the British evangelical constituency went into deep shock when one of its foremost preachers, teachers and intellectuals, the minister of the Eden Baptist Church in Cambridge, announced that he was leaving his wife and family to live with a homosexual partner. Evangelicals offered prayer and sympathy – though it was often a qualified sympathy. It was hoped that the minister could come to admit his sin, repent of it and be reconciled again to his fellow Christians. There was little sympathy for the dilemma with which he had been living: to be homosexual among a group of people who regarded this as a matter of choice, wilful disobedience towards God's law. His decision to resolve the situation inevitably dealt the cause of conservative evangelicalism a serious blow, especially as it became clear that the minister had struggled with homosexual tendencies over many years, and this suggested that there might be other clergy who were living with aspects of their personality deeply suppressed if not denied. In the twenty-first century many would regard this as psychologically unhealthy.

The prioritization of the conversion experience can lead evangelical clergy to be impatient with non-evangelicals and look to create networks of support of the like-minded rather than among those in their local deaneries or circuits. They then expend less effort making the formal structures of their denomination work. This weakens the sense of solidarity among their fellow but non-evangelical clergy and can become an occasion for resentment. In this sense they are church minimalists, often suspicious of church bureaucracy. When did bureaucracy ever convert anyone? The doctrine of the Church is not high on their list of teachings. The Alpha course, for example, which was one of the very few successful evangelistic courses to come out of the Decade of Evangelism, is scarcely interested in the Church in any institutional sense.

Evangelicalism understands itself as a movement rather than an institution. The point about a movement is that it moves – it moves out of parochial structures to plant new congregations; it moves out of church buildings to present the gospel in whatever places people congregate; it moves across the world to take the saving message.

Similarly, many evangelicals are lukewarm in their support of the ecumenical movement, despite the more positive commitment at the 1967 Keele Conference of evangelicals. They happily cross denominational boundaries and work with fellow evangelicals in other churches, but they can be reluctant to join with non-evangelicals. In interfaith matters – which is a key contribution that the churches can make to social and community cohesion for the future – they are generally wary and sometimes hostile towards attempts to bring the faiths together, especially if some form of joint prayer or worship is suggested.

Although evangelicals have a commendable record of social concern historically (William Wilberforce and the anti-slavery campaigners, Lord Shaftesbury and factory reform), in the twentieth century this social witness was not high among evangelical priorities. The situation has changed in more recent years, not least in the United States where, for example, Jim Wallis formed a congregation of evangelicals for social justice in Washington, DC. But there is often a reluctance to join with those who are not evangelical Christians or not Christians.

Evangelicals have a love–hate relationship with scholarship and the academic world. There are some fine evangelical scholars, but they are not always appreciated by their fellow evangelical Christians. Since the gospel is communicated by the Holy Spirit directly to the heart of the receptive individual, be he wise or simple, there is often scepticism about the value of putting the Scriptures into the hands of 'experts'. Why subject God's word to the criteria of the academy? As a result, many congregations struggle to hold members whose intellectual curiosity takes them beyond the reading material found in most evangelical churches. Yet a diet of C. S. Lewis and John Stott can only take you so far. More particularly, it leaves the children of committed evangelicals at a considerable disadvantage when they begin to encounter the cultured despisers of religion in school and at university.

Evangelical worship also has its limitations. It is joyful, it is lively, it is exuberant and it is easily accessible. The words and the music used in worship require little intellectual effort. But the range and depth of emotions that are appealed to is often limited. Certain moods are not encouraged and important aspects of human life – doubt, disbelief, despair, sadness – can be treated somewhat superficially as a result. The dominant note is always happiness because to know the Lord as your personal saviour is a cause for gratitude and happiness. But for some people, 'A little talk with Jesus' does not necessarily or easily make it 'right, all right'. In charismatic congregations, where singing and praying can be highly expressive – calling out, raising arms – it can be experienced as quite coercive, especially by those whose personalities respond more to quiet thoughtfulness – or those who are simply shy. If you don't want to spoil the party you may have to stay away.

In one further respect the evangelical movement is as out of step with the vast majority of contemporary citizens as it is with many other non-evangelical Christians: attitudes towards gender and the role of women. Those outside the Church (as well as many within) see sexual equality as one of the most significant ethical issues of our time and cannot accept that biblical texts are incapable of fresh interpretation in the light of contemporary knowledge about sexuality and sexual orientation. Opposition to practising homosexuals is not confined to the evangelical wing of the Church, but evangelicals do exercise considerable influence on the Church's stated position. In addition, opposition to women's ordination is resulting in the strange phenomenon of some evangelical women having to seek ordination without the sponsorship of their own congregations and then ministering in churches that are not in their theological tradition, which inevitably puts some psychological strain on them.

Conclusion

The evangelical minister has every right in the modern Church to demand that his form of Christian ministry is given greater attention, because the only churches that are growing in any numbers are those that receive the ministry of evangelical clergy. But this approach tends to take congregations away from the inclusivist model of the classical Anglican church and towards the more exclusivist model of the associational type of congregation. Yet Anglican evangelicals have historically set great store by the principles of the Book of Common Prayer, and one of these is a commitment to be as inclusive as possible – a necessary stance for a Church that seeks to be the nation's chaplain. There is something unresolved here to which we shall need to return because how it is resolved will determine the future of the Church of England if not other churches.

But perhaps the most important contribution that evangelicals can make to the future ordained ministry comes from their commitment to careful teaching. The Church in Britain has rather lazily assumed that the Christian faith will be communicated to the next generation primarily through parental example and then through religious education in schools. As a consequence it has scandalously neglected the nurture of several generations of children as the Sunday School movement was allowed to atrophy and die from the 1960s onwards, and insufficient attention was paid to the likely consequences of changes to religious education syllabuses and the collective act of worship over the same period. But religion has virtually disappeared from the home, religious education syllabuses are no longer concerned exclusively with teaching Christianity, and few schoolchildren now experience worship. As a consequence, Christian intellectual capital is depleting rapidly in a country that is ceasing to be even nominally Christian. This is curious since for many people it is precisely at the point that they become responsible for the care and nurture of children that they start to think seriously again about the claims and values of Christianity; the faith school has never been so popular. The Church needs to say, prophetically, that future generations will not grow up in a vacuum. If they are not rooted from the beginning of their lives in a moral community they will be at the mercy of whatever influences are dominant in the society in which they grow up. The Church needs the evangelicals to say this.

5

Catholic: the priest

The poor understood the meaning of sacrificial love – and men like Lowder, Goulden, Mackonochie, Stanton, and Talbot lived long enough among them that they could not fail to recognise its presence.

Desmond Bowen

Tractarian spirituality disliked what was flamboyant. It shrank from religion in the market-square ... Religion was very sacred, too sacred to be cast among swine.

Owen Chadwick

Origins and evolution

From the last decades of the nineteenth century until the Second World War, the catholic movement within the Church of England grew in confidence and influence – so much so that its model of ordained ministry came to dominate Anglican thinking and practice. This is not to say that most clergy were committed Anglo-Catholics; they were not. But even those who were not of the catholic party were influenced by the example of the catholic priests and the theology of priesthood on which it was based. Part of the reason for this was that Anglo-Catholicism was above all a movement of the parish clergy. Initially at any rate, the bishops were lukewarm and the laity was suspicious. Anglo-Catholicism gave to parochial clergy the assurance they needed at a time when their confidence was being undermined by a growing marginalization of the Christian Church, particularly the Church of England, in the expanding industrial cities of Victorian and Edwardian England. The complacent assumption of the national Church that everyone was somehow a member of the Church of England by virtue of being English, left the clergy of a hitherto mainly rural Church unprepared for the cold climate of the more secular city. Although it would be untrue and unfair to say that there had been no revival of parish ministry before the catholic movement, those priests who embraced Anglo-Catholicism set to work confident in the knowledge that while they might be ordained ministers of an erastian Church (see page 65), they were first of all priests of the Church of Jesus Christ and as such had a mission that originated with the Lord himself. This confidence was reinforced by the fact that they were 'anglo' as well as 'catholic' priests – circumstance and theology worked together. The Church of England, with its historic commitment to the whole nation and its parochial organization, was presented with potential opportunities for mission and ministry that were denied other Christian bodies. Anglo-Catholic clergy would minister to the people of England by being *parish priests* in a *national* Church.

The origins of Anglo-Catholicism

The catholic movement began in clerical and academic circles in Oxford in the 1830s. While Keble, Newman and Pusey gave it its essential theological underpinning (at first in a series of Tracts for the Times – hence the name 'Tractarians'), after Newman's departure for the Roman Catholic Church in 1845, clergy were increasingly inspired by the example of catholic clergy in towns and cities across the country: Lowder at London Docks, Mackonochie of St Alban's Holborn, Wagner in Brighton, Prynne in Oxford, Ommanney in Sheffield, Bell Cox in Liverpool, and so on. Much of what they did now seems rather obvious and undramatic; but for a sleeping Church it was a revelation to see clergy introduce evening services, carefully prepare candidates for confirmation, urge people to make more frequent Communions, give devotional talks in Lent, visit the laity systematically, hold classes for communicants and set up guilds for servers. Father Lowder, who went to work at St George in the East in 1856, has left this account of a typical day for the staff in the Parochial Mission House:

> The first bell for rising was rung at 6.30am; we said Prime in the Oratory at 7; Mattins was said at 7.30, followed by the celebration of the Holy Eucharist. After breakfast, followed by Terce, the clergy and teachers went to their respective work – some in school, some in the study or district. Sext was said at 12.45, immediately before dinner, when the household again assembled . . . After dinner, rest, letters, visiting, or school work, as the case might be, and then tea at 5.30. After tea, choir practice, classes, hearing confessions, or attending to special cases. Supper at 9.15, followed by Compline, when those who had finished their work returned to their rooms.[1]

Anglo-Catholic parish priests were above all busy!

The Anglo-Catholic style of worship became more elaborate, more ritualistic, more Roman Catholic, as the years passed. The Eucharist was celebrated in vestments, the altar adorned with six standing candles and a crucifix, the Blessed Sacrament was reserved in an aumbry (a wall safe) and then a tabernacle (on the altar). There were processions; there were hanging lamps; there were elaborate rood screens; there were colourful banners; there were stations of the cross; there was incense; there were gongs and bells. All the senses were engaged. Some have seen this as an attempt to give the people of the slums, whose working lives were spent in the dark satanic mills of industrial Britain, a foretaste of heaven. Others see it as part of a much wider movement in later Victorian society that wanted to turn its back on the industrial revolution, the age of the machine, and escape into a medieval fantasy world where life was uncomplicated and lived closer to nature – and when the Church was at the centre of it all.

The golden age

The highpoint was probably the inter-war period of the Anglo-Catholic Congresses – huge gatherings of clergy from across the country. It is hard to realize now just how confident Anglo-Catholic priests were at this time, though this extract from a speech at the close of the first Anglo-Catholic Priests' Convention in Oxford in 1921 gives a flavour of the mood. The overall theme of the convention was 'Priestly efficiency', and towards the close of it Father Briscoe spoke about the missional task of the Church of England. He saw this as nothing less than 'the evangelization of England' with the priests – the laity are not mentioned – as 'the instruments and agents for this tremendous work':

> It is to no less a work that our Lord has called us: it was for no less a purpose that the Bishop laid his hands on us when he made us Priests. Tonight we assure ourselves afresh of the reality, the validity, the security of our glorious mission . . . We alone can do it. The national Church alone has the freedom of access everywhere, the command of attention, the hold on the affections of our people which give the opportunity for the appeal of God to be effectively made.[2]

He went on to tell the assembled clergy that the evangelization of England required great personal sacrifice on their part. They had to attempt to 'live like the saints'. Such a life, 'plainly consecrated to God, a life of loneliness, of prayer, of work' would be more eloquent than any sermon. This exhortation was able to galvanize Father Briscoe's audience because they already shared the same model of Anglican ordained ministry.

It has been claimed that the catholic movement created a new ideal of the Church's ministry and a new type of clergyman, but in the judgement of Canon W. J. Sparrow Simpson, writing at the time of the movement's centenary in 1933, it would be more accurate to say that it 'restored to the English Church an ancient but almost forgotten ideal'. Simpson described this as 'the recovery of consciousness that the Christian minister was not only a prophet but a priest'.[3] The catholic revival was in large measure about the recovery of the more sacerdotal aspects of priesthood. This involved Anglo-Catholics reaching back into Church history, behind three hundred years of a more Protestant past, behind the Reformation, to the medieval and early Church. Essentially, they sought the renewal and reform of the Church of England by an appeal not to how things might be in the future but to how things had been in the past – though this was often a rather idealized past.

The model

What, then, was their theology of ordained ministry? Three major areas of doctrine were foundational for the Anglo-Catholic understanding of the Church, its nature and mission, and the role of the ordained minister.

The Church of England and the Church of Jesus

First, the Church of England was understood as part of the one, holy, catholic and apostolic Church founded by Jesus Christ and perpetuated in history through episcopal ordination. This was the subject of the first of the Tracts for the Times: 'On what are the clergy to rest their authority when the state deserts them? Upon nothing else than their apostolic descent.' In making this assertion Anglo-Catholics were faced with opponents from two different directions – Anglican and Roman Catholic. There were two sorts of Anglican who were suspicious of the claims of the catholics. On the one hand, there were those, mainly evangelical, who were not persuaded that the Church and its ordained ministry was ever anything other than a human arrangement (a view shared by many Nonconformists), a gathering together of the like-minded or a fellowship of the elect. On the other, there were thoroughgoing erastians who viewed the Church as the religious arm of the state and the clergy as a kind of religious civil service deriving their authority not from Christ but the crown.

The evangelicals generally believed the Church could exist in any number of arrangements according to circumstance. W. H. Griffiths Thomas, for example, a distinguished Principal of the evangelical theological college, Wycliffe Hall, taught ordinands that the ordained ministry had developed (quite properly) from the rather different pattern of ministry found in the New Testament under the pressure of circumstances. He also insisted that the Church *was* a priesthood rather than *had* a priesthood, and that all baptized Christians exercised a valuable ministry; the ordained were not privileged or special.[4] Against these views Anglo-Catholics insisted that the Church originated with the commission of Jesus and that, in the words of Newman, 'Every bishop of the Church whom we behold, is a lineal descendant of St Peter and St Paul after the order of a spiritual birth', and that the threefold order of bishop, priest and deacon could be traced to the New Testament itself.[5] We could say that catholics thought of the Church as part of the gospel whereas for evangelicals the Church was the bearer of it.

Those Anglicans who held erastian views were challenged to recognize the Church as a divine society as well as a human organization. This was the burden of John Keble's Assize sermon in Oxford in 1833, which is generally held to be the start of the catholic movement within the Church. The sermon attacked the government of the day over a relatively trivial issue: a proposal to suppress ten Irish bishoprics. But Keble saw this as symptomatic of an erastian Church whose clergy thought of themselves as government functionaries. The Oxford reformers asserted instead that while the Church of England may have been created by Act of Parliament, the holy catholic Church, of which the English Church was a part, was not a creature of government but a divine society instituted by the Lord himself. As such it had its own proper autonomy.

At the same time, the Anglo-Catholics had to meet the criticisms of the Roman Catholic Church that in 1896 had declared Anglican orders 'absolutely null and utterly void'.[6] There were two main reasons for Roman objections. The first was that the apostolic succession through the laying on of hands had been broken at the time of Archbishop Matthew Parker (1504–75) and the Elizabethan Church. It was alleged that Parker was not validly consecrated. Against this it was argued that even if this were so, the tactile succession had been restored with Archbishop Laud (1573–1645), who was consecrated by bishops whose succession was not disputed. The second objection was that the intention of the Anglican Ordinal was defective in that the priesthood is not conceived as a sacrificing priesthood. The Archbishops of Canterbury and York countered this objection in an Encyclical Letter by saying that the intention of the Church of England in ordination was to confer on its priests everything that Christ had intended.[7] If the Anglican Ordinal was defective because it did not speak of a sacrificing priesthood in so many words, it was little different from the forms of ordination used at earlier periods in the Church's long history and from which contemporary Roman Catholic orders ultimately derived.

The spiritual authority of the priest

The second area of doctrine on which the Anglo-Catholic theology of ordained ministry rested was the idea of priestly vocation. Anglo-Catholics argued that the authority of the Anglican priest did not derive from the fact that the Church of England was the national Church – for it might not always enjoy such status – but from the clergyman's call by God and his ordination as a priest in the Church of Jesus Christ. Although the Church had a duty to foster vocations and then to select, train and ordain men, all that the Church was doing was recognizing the call of God. The ultimate authority of the priest in spiritual matters lay in his call by God and the resources of grace he needed for his work that were poured out upon him by the Holy Spirit at ordination. The priest was authorized and empowered to celebrate the sacrament of Holy Communion (which catholics understood as the re-presentation of Christ's sacrificial death on the cross), to bestow God's blessing and to grant absolution to the penitent sinner (Anglo-Catholics restored confession before a priest in the Church of England); none of which lay persons could do.

Holiness and the salvation of souls

The third crucial doctrine that Anglo-Catholics had at the centre of their teaching was the need for salvation and the living of a holy life. The two are connected: the person who is saved lives a holy life; the one who lives a holy life is saved. The title of the first of Newman's *Parochial and Plain Sermons* is explicit: 'Holiness without which no man shall see the Lord'. Although catholic clergy were involved in many parochial activities both religious and secular, they never lost sight of the fact that their primary objective was the salvation of individual souls and making people holy. This was well summarized in a sermon that Dr H. P. Liddon preached on behalf of St George's Mission in 1860:

> The Mission has not attempted the mere civilisation of the many. It has attempted the actual *salvation* of some ... The clergy live in the centre of a dense population ... They are surrounding themselves with services, schools, reformatories. They are winning penitents, and gathering in communicants. Their object is not merely to diffuse an influence, but, in the Name and by the strength of Christ, to save.[8]

Clergy, therefore, had to have a concern for people as individuals, for it is only individuals who can repent and be saved. 'The good shepherd', they were fond of reminding themselves, 'calls his own sheep by name'.[9] Knowing the sheep required the clergy to visit people in their homes. Anglican clergy had always felt under some obligation to visit, though widespread non-residence until the later part of the nineteenth century meant that it was one of the more neglected duties. In previous centuries it had often been no more than a matter of social convention: the minor gentry, to which the clergy belonged, visited each other socially and visited the poor to bestow charity – *noblesse oblige*. Visiting was now with the express purpose of getting to know individual worshippers well in order to encourage them in their Christian life and become a friend to them. The slum priest knew well that working-class people would not turn to the clergy for pastoral help or spiritual advice unless a friendly relationship had already been established. Catholic clergy also believed that 'being saved' involved more than a once-for-all experience; it required the cultivation of habits of prayer and worship over a lifetime of faithful discipleship – in short, a holy life. They were, therefore, ready for the long haul with people and often stayed in parishes for substantial periods of time.

The centrality of the Eucharist

Men and women were to be saved and made holy through grace. Grace was made available to the worshipper through the sacraments, which were channels of grace. The sacraments included confession before a priest – though it is doubtful whether priests were ever able to persuade the majority of their congregations to go to confession. While not everyone made individual confession, all catholics were expected to be at mass every Sunday and on the Church's red-letter days (major festivals). Receiving regularly the sacrament of Christ's body and blood was both the heart of worship and the means of sanctification.

Anglo-Catholics believed that the Lord was objectively present in the consecrated elements of bread and wine. This was not a commitment to the Roman Catholic doctrine of transubstantiation – though some did teach this – but to belief in the real presence of Christ in the sacrament. In Newman's words:

> He who is at the right hand of God, manifests Himself in that Holy Sacrament as really as if He were visibly there. We are allowed to draw near, to 'give, take, and eat' His sacred Body and Blood, as truly as though like Thomas we could touch His hands and thrust our hand into His side.[10]

This was Christ's chosen means of 'conveying to our hearts and bodies His own gracious self'.[11] This is the theme of many of the Communion hymns that catholic hymn books contain. Canon Sparrow Simpson's hymn 'All for Jesus!' (in Stainer's *Crucifixion*) is a good example:

> All for Jesus! at thine altar
> Thou dost give us sweet content;
> There, dear Saviour, we receive thee
> In thy holy sacrament.

Catholics believed that when the priest recited the prayer of consecration, the sacrificial death of Christ on the cross was not just called to mind but made real, made present, at the altar. This is clearly expressed in William Bright's Communion hymn:

> And now, O Father, mindful of the love
> That bought us once for all, on Calvary's tree,
> And having with us him that pleads above,
> We here present, we here spread forth to thee
> That only offering perfect in thine eyes,
> The one true, pure immortal sacrifice.

The priest does not sacrifice Christ again (the Roman doctrine); he re-presents the once-and-for-all sacrifice of Christ on Calvary. It is in this sense that the Anglican priesthood is to be understood as a sacrificing priesthood. Accordingly, many catholics spoke of the Eucharist as 'offering the holy sacrifice'. Of course some Anglo-Catholic priests adopted the Roman Catholic doctrine of the mass – repeated sacrifice, transubstantiation. But these doctrinal positions were expressly rejected by the Church of England in the Articles of Religion.[12]

Christ's presence was an objective presence, in no way dependent on the spiritual state of the worshipper (or for that matter the worthiness of the priest), and this was reinforced for worshippers by the practice of genuflecting towards the consecrated elements. The communicant approached the altar to receive the sacrament, therefore, with a mixture of awe and confidence. Awareness of the divine presence was the life-giving and life-changing moment of catholic spiritual experience. At this moment in the liturgy the worshipper's whole attention was given to the adoration and reception of the Lord present in the sacrament of his body and blood. At this moment the penitent and forgiven sinner knew that he or she was caught up in that communion with the Lord that alone satisfied the longing soul and the restless heart. At this moment the worshipper knew that he had received those resources of grace that he needed to sustain him in the week ahead.

Not surprisingly, Anglo-Catholic priests pressed for more frequent Communion in a Church that had been guilty of considerable neglect of its Lord's command to 'do this in remembrance of me'. The Oxford reformers were content to restore a weekly celebration after centuries of infrequent Communion, though in the later nineteenth century and the early decades of the twentieth, a daily celebration became the goal of many catholic clergy. In some more Roman-inclined parishes the main Eucharist of the day on Sunday was High Mass, at which only the priest received the sacrament, hidden in a cloud of incense before the altar. This practice displeased the Anglo-Catholic liturgical scholar,

A. G. Hebert, who lamented in 1929 that it was one of the failures of the catholic revival that 'it has not succeeded in restoring the communion of the people as an integral part of the chief mass on a Sunday'.[13] But as the century progressed, non-communicating masses gave way to a Parish Mass or Parish Communion with greater direct congregational involvement in increasing numbers of parishes, not least as a result of Hebert's own writing.[14] Something was gained in the process – the sense of belonging to the body, the communitarian dimension – though something was also lost – the sense of mystery. Such was the influence of the catholic movement across the Anglican spectrum that the Parish Communion came to displace sung matins as well. As a result, Anglican worship became increasingly sacramental and communicant figures rose consistently throughout the early decades of the twentieth century, masking for a while the fact that overall numbers of people drawn into the life of the church were falling. The move to a more sacramental church had other effects as well. It alienated those Anglicans who preferred a non-eucharistic form of worship, it made it more difficult for the occasional attender and it emphasized the role of the priest within the Christian community, since only priests could absolve and celebrate Communion.

The stress on holiness was the main reason why the saints' days were marked by celebrations of Holy Communion and the faithful encouraged to attend. Here were examples of men and women from each age of the Christian past who had lived lives of exceptional holiness, often, as with the martyrs, in the most hostile or difficult circumstances. These people were to be emulated, for all Christians should strive to make their lives holy.

Priesthood and ontological change

Finally, catholics understood priesthood in ontological rather than functional terms. It was a matter of what a priest *was* as much as what he *did*. God did not call people who had certain aptitudes to undertake a range of tasks in his Church; he called people to be transformed into priests, to undergo a profound change by acquiring the priestly character. This was why the priestly vocation was a vocation for life. If being a priest were simply about performing tasks, these could be picked up or set down. But once a priest, always a priest – the 'indelibility of orders'. This unique vocation together with a form of training that was concerned with the person's entire development – 'priestly formation' – and a lifetime of being shaped and fashioned by the priestly disciplines of the daily office and eucharistic celebration, put the emphasis firmly on what the priest was as much as what the priest did. There was a conscious attempt to fashion a particular type of personality. The theological underpinning of this was the idea of incarnation. As God had become human in Jesus Christ in order to engage with human beings, clergy had to adopt a similar, incarnational style of ministry – being present with people.

I have said that Anglo-Catholic clergy were busy, and they were. But this 'doing' flowed from this 'being'. Moreover, it was the knowledge that they were priests that could sustain them when the busyness produced exhaustion, as it frequently did, or when their activity seemed to show few tangible results. Later generations of clergy who copied the activism but forgot or knew nothing of the need for whole lives to be steeped in catholic disciplines could not sustain their ministries when the going became hard.

These foundational beliefs about the Church and a more sacerdotal understanding of ordained ministry were fundamental in restoring to parish clergy a sense of their significance and worth, not only in the face of a more secular world but also over against their most successful religious rivals in the towns – the Free Church ministers. It is highly likely that attendance at Free Churches exceeded attendance at Anglican in the second half of the nineteenth century.[15] The theology of Anglo-Catholicism reassured the clergy of the established Church by showing that there was a world of difference between belonging to the Free Churches and belonging to the Church of England. The Church of England had maintained the historic link with the medieval and primitive Church through episcopal ordination (the apostolic succession): the terms 'minister' and 'priest' were not interchangeable. Evangelism was given a new cutting edge.

The pastoral ideal

As well as having a more sacerdotal theology of priesthood, two other features of Anglo-Catholic practice are crucial parts of their model of ordained ministry.

First, we have already noticed how energetic catholic clergy were. Their lives were not to be lived out at some leisurely pace, for they saw themselves as the principal (if not the only) pastors to their flocks. They determined to fulfil that part of the Ordinal that emphasizes the shepherding role of the priest, for saving and caring went hand in hand. It was their task

> ... to feed and provide for the Lord's family; to seek for Christ's sheep that are dispersed abroad, and for his children who are in the midst of this naughty world, that they may be saved through Christ for ever.[16]

The priest modelled his ministry on that of Jesus Christ. It was 'incarnational'. Jesus lived among the people to whom he ministered and concerned

himself with all facets of their lives. For many pre-Second World War
catholic clergy the idea of 'incarnational' ministry had a further dimension to it, for they were often from more privileged social backgrounds
and came to their working-class parishes at some social cost.[17] They might
not have come down from heaven but they certainly came down the
ladder of social class. Incarnational ministry in the context of the parish
system required the priest to devote himself to all the people of his
geographical parish, and not just his congregation, though especially
the deprived and needy. He had to busy himself with the totality of
their concerns, however mundane or secular, though always with an eye
to their souls. Where Jesus had healed the leper and fed the hungry,
the slum priest befriended the workers in the sweat shops and led the
campaign for better housing. This approach was well summarized in a
speech by one of the great saints of the catholic movement, Frank Weston,
Bishop of Zanzibar, at the second Anglo-Catholic Congress in 1923. In
earnest tone the Bishop said to a packed Albert Hall:

> You cannot claim to worship Jesus in the tabernacle if you do not pity
> Jesus in the slum ...You have your Mass, you have your altars, you
> have begun to get your tabernacles. Now go out into the highways
> and hedges, and look for Jesus in the ragged and the naked, in the
> oppressed and the sweated, in those who have lost hope, and in
> those who are struggling to make good. Look for Jesus in them;
> and, when you have found Him, gird yourself with His towel of
> fellowship and wash His feet in the person of His brethren.[18]

It was said of these priests that they were as interested in the direction of
sewers as of souls. One effect of this was to draw some of them towards
the politics of social amelioration. These were also the days before the
advent of television, when churches still provided a wide range of social
activities for parishioners, many of which were either run by or regularly
visited by the parish clergy. Given the wide range of their concerns, it
is not surprising that Canon Peter Green, describing a typical Sunday
in 1922, wrote of returning to supper 'too tired to eat'.[19]

As well as being pastors, Anglo-Catholic priests were also teachers.
Indeed, they would probably say that one of the most important ways
in which they were able to offer pastoral support to people was through
sound teaching. What they taught was not Christianity in some generalized and non-denominational sense (in the way that the state schools
would teach it after 1945) but the catholic faith of the Church of
England. They taught people to observe the liturgical year, to receive
sacramental grace by attending mass every Sunday and on saints' days,
to practise self-examination and fasting before receiving Communion,
to make confession regularly before a priest, to pray every day to our

Lord and our Lady, to make a retreat or a pilgrimage once each year and so on. They went to their parishes knowing full well what it meant to 'build up a congregation': it was to teach the faith and practice of catholicism. Teaching began with quite small children. Even as late as 1952, Joseph Williamson (Father Joe) recounts in his autobiography how he began his work at St Paul's, Dock Street, with children:

> So I taught these children to sing Mass to the music of Merbeck, in faith that the repetition of the words of worship, confession and prayer would bring something to life in the heart and soul of some Stepney boy or girl, as they did for me in Poplar many years ago.[20]

The catholic clergy taught with enormous self-assurance. Kingsley Martin, the journalist, observed Conrad Noel at Thaxted and noted that he 'spoke with unassumed authority, for he spoke as a priest'.[21] However, this self-confidence had other roots as well. Some Anglo-Catholic clergy had the self-assurance of those who came from a privileged social background. Others were individualists to a marked degree, certain of their own rightness. This sometimes resulted in eccentricities of behaviour. Father Lowndes, for example, said mass in Latin and denounced the Book of Common Prayer as a work of the devil; Father Briscoe believed all clergy should be celibate and sought to separate priests from their wives![22] Nevertheless, apart from the odd eccentricity, the commitment to teaching was faithfully observed and central to the work of all catholic clergy. Consequently, members of their congregations knew what it was to be a catholic Anglican and knew the points at which it was different from both other forms of Christianity in general and Anglicanism in particular.

The model in practice

The collapse of the catholic movement has been even swifter than its rise. In the 1920s its leading figures were full of optimism and confidence. By the 1950s this was fast disappearing due to a combination of theology and circumstance. Changes in theology undermined the catholic model of priest, changes in British society after the Second World War made the decline of the catholic constituency more likely.

Major theological changes came from biblical and historical studies into the origins, nature and mission of the Church. As we saw in Chapter 2, there was a shift from seeing the Church primarily as an institution hierarchically organized to seeing it as the pilgrim people of God, journeying towards that kingdom that Jesus initiated but whose consummation lay in the mysterious future. This image of a people on the move, constantly having to change and adapt to new circumstances, made it very difficult to think of the Church in fixed institutional terms. What we see in the pages of the New Testament is an abundance of images and a process of change and adaptation.[23] At the same time, all the churches recovered what seemed to be one constant image running through all the New Testament writings: the idea of the whole people of God, lay and ordained, as a priesthood in which every baptized person and not just the ordained had a vocation.

But in any case, the traditional model of priest worked less well in the sort of society that emerged in Britain after 1945. Within the Church, the laity were universally better educated than they had ever been before, which made more paternalistic modes of being a minister seem anachronistic. Even before the war one catholic writer had noted that 'Men and women are almost everywhere less simple, less docile, more critical than they were.'[24] Greater and greater numbers of lay people received education at levels that were at least as high if not higher than those of many clergy. Clergy had to learn how to work in partnership with a more articulate laity and to recognize that in some areas lay people had greater wisdom, experience and ability than them. In addition, the rise of the welfare professionals challenged the clergy as pastors in the wider community. Fewer and fewer people looked to the clergy for pastoral help, preferring instead to go to those who seemed to have greater knowledge and expertise. As the nation became more plural, questions arose about the extent to which a Christian minister could be a pastor to people who no longer shared the basic assumptions of the Christian faith.

Some Anglo-Catholic priests compensated for loss of status as clergy by engaging in activities that did seem to have social usefulness. During the 1960s, inner-city clergy in particular became in effect social workers and, later, community workers. Some were politicized during the years of the Thatcher governments (as was the Church of England more generally) and were involved in local government as Labour and Liberal Party activists or local councillors. When fashions had changed in the 1970s, others had become counsellors or therapists. These are themes I shall take up in the next chapter.

Other factors also weakened the Anglo-Catholic constituency. In the first place, Anglo-Catholic congregations were easier to create and sustain where communities were relatively settled and lay people were willing to give a large proportion of their time to churchgoing over many years. It took time to be a catholic; there was so much to learn! Congregations had to be trained in catholic doctrine and practice. To feel comfortable in worship, for example, required mastery of complex liturgies and ritual with considerable seasonal variation. Moreover, to perform these acts of worship well demanded servers and choirs with extensive repertoires. But the history of post-war England was a history of people on the move. Inner-city, working-class communities were broken up and rehoused. Young people began to receive good state education and left for better jobs or universities, never to return to the churches of their youth. Catholic-minded clergy in the new housing areas, faced with congregations from a variety of church backgrounds, tended to become more 'middle of the road' in order to make worship more accessible. They were influenced by the liturgical movement that had as the main act of worship on Sunday a Family or Parish Communion as recommended by Father Hebert. The clergy might retain catholic externals – vestments, candles, aumbries, ceremonial – but this was not always accompanied by the systematic and sustained teaching of catholic doctrine. When the Alternative Service Book appeared in 1980, much of the catholic ritual tended to disappear as well.

Then, in the second place, the Anglo-Catholic constituency was never a majority of the Church, so that its numbers were considerably reduced as a result of the general decline in church attendance. Congregations were also threatened by the fact that many of them were in slum parishes that were subject to considerable demolition and redevelopment in the post-war period. As a result, Anglo-Catholic worshippers were scattered and found themselves in non-catholic parishes. By the time of the movement's one hundred and fiftieth anniversary mass in Oxford in 1983, it was painfully obvious that the membership that remained was ageing. Young people searching for more vibrant worship and more immediate religious experience now found it – if they found it in the Church at all – not in Anglo-Catholicism but in charismatic evangelicalism. Those who looked for a fulfilling career in pastoral work turned to the social and welfare services of the state.

Finally, the catholic movement was fatally weakened by its own internal divisions which, whatever the specific issue, seemed to come back sooner or later to the question of authority. Where did final authority lie in a Church that, unlike the Roman Catholic Church, did not teach the infallibility of either bishops or synods and always tried to embrace a range of theological opinions? The issue had been stirred repeatedly throughout the movement's history by the publication of a series of books – *Essays and Reviews* (1860), *Lux Mundi* (1889) and *Essays Catholic and Critical* (1927) – by those liberal catholics who believed the human mind had to be open to the claims of truth wherever they might lead, even if that meant challenging some of the received wisdom. Traditionalists feared that the authority of Scripture and the Church was being surrendered to what, in the end, and however scholarly, would be purely private judgements. At the beginning of the twentieth century the liberal catholics tended to produce the more vigorous scholars and were increasingly influential. By the middle decades of the century, the majority of catholic-minded clergy were probably liberal in theology even if more conservative liturgically: security could not be had in the changing world of critical scholarship but it could be had in the more stable world of the Church's liturgy. However, some theological issues also directly affected church practice. The proposal to ordain women to the priesthood forced liberal and conservative catholics to declare themselves, and the movement was fractured irreparably.

Those who opposed the ordination of women often did so by making a contrast between those who, in the words of E. L. Mascall, a distinguished Anglo-Catholic scholar, 'believe in the fundamentally revealed and given character of the Christian religion and those who find their norms in the outlook and assumptions of contemporary secularized culture and are concerned to assimilate the beliefs and institutions of Christianity to it'.[25] Although this is what many Anglo-Catholics firmly believed, they could only do so by ignoring the theological arguments mounted by the proponents of women's ordination. Those who wanted to see women ordained believed they had won the theological debate.

The theological argument centred around two questions: Could women be ordained in principle? and: Did the Church of England have the authority to ordain them? Other arguments were largely pragmatic, to do with the wisdom of pressing ahead at this moment in time: Would it damage relations with other churches, especially the Roman Catholic and Orthodox Churches? Were members of the Church of England ready for it?[26] On the question of timing, catholics had no more wisdom than anyone else. But it was hard to resist those who argued that if something were theologically sound, pragmatic arguments or simple gut reactions should not be allowed to stand in the way.

The objection in principle to women being ordained was often posed by Anglo-Catholics in this way: Could a woman represent Jesus Christ at the altar? Accepting for a moment this way of thinking about the priest (as an icon of Jesus Christ himself), the issue turned on just what it was that the priest at the altar, breaking the bread and blessing the wine, was meant to call to mind or represent. The theological answer was that the priest represented the One who by becoming human became the saviour of all humanity, male and female. The significant aspect of the incarnation was the taking of human flesh, not the assumption of a particular gender. The fact that Jesus was male had no more soteriological significance than that he was Jewish or a carpenter or dark-skinned. The priest at the altar called to mind his humanity, not his gender or his race or his occupation. (A Eucharist is not like a nativity play, which seeks to reproduce a historical family – though even school nativity plays may feature a white mother and a black baby without causing too much theological distress.) Indeed, since Christ died for all, there was a strong argument for saying that the priesthood was better able to be iconic of Christ if it could embrace people of each gender and every race.

But did the Church of England have authority to ordain women when the majority of Christians did not do so? This was perhaps the weakest argument of all. If the Church of England did not have authority to make decisions about church order, it was hard to see how it was ever able to assume authority for breaking from Rome in the first place. As so often in the brief history of Anglo-Catholicism, an issue about something else led back to the question of authority, and some discovered to their surprise that they had never really thought it through before.

Catholics split three ways over the ordination of women: some left for other churches, principally the Roman Catholic Church, though some became Orthodox; others remained within the Anglican Church but opposed to women priests; others embraced the concept, some reluctantly (feeling the time was not ripe), some wholeheartedly. The movement ceased to be united and many catholics were left bruised if not bitter – a spectacle that was hardly likely to set the world on fire. Nor did it.

Strengths and weaknesses

When we look at the present state of the catholic movement in the Church of England it is hard not to conclude that it is in terminal decline. However, the tradition has exercised a powerful influence in the recent past and still influences members of the Church. We need to be clear about its particular strengths and weaknesses.

The strengths

When the catholic movement began in the nineteenth century, Anglican clergy throughout the country were unsettled by the pace of momentous economic and cultural change going on around them. Priests within the catholic movement were equipped with both a coherent theology of ordained ministry and also examples of good practice: they had a model of ministry. This gave them the confidence they needed to sustain long, sometimes lonely, and always demanding ministries in the rapidly expanding cities of Victorian and Edwardian England. They were reassured about their professional status as other occupational groups professionalized, and enabled to respond to the vigorous competition they faced from the Free Churches in the period before the First World War. Moreover, in many respects they had a model of ministry that other clergy who were not Anglo-Catholic could in some measure emulate. A sung Eucharist became the norm for Anglican Sunday worship, and the pastoral activities of catholic clergy were widely copied.

At the heart of catholic ordained ministry was the conviction that the priestly task of the Church was to save souls and to help men and women lead holy lives by means of sacramental grace within the context of the Christian community. This was the goal of all parochial activity and the final test of every priest's work. In this sense the catholic movement at its best was evangelical at heart (many of the early Tractarians had been evangelicals). While their language might differ, both catholics and evangelicals knew about the need for personal conversion. In particular, catholic priests knew the power of worship to move hearts; they made good worship the absolute priority of their ministries. In this lay the strength of Anglo-Catholicism. This ought to be the movement's lasting gift to the coming Church.

The weaknesses

But the Anglo-Catholic model had serious weaknesses and these were increasingly exposed after the Second World War, until by the 1960s some refinements of the model if not alternative models were sorely needed.

First, the catholic paradigm of the Church and the ordained ministry was thoroughly clerical and had the effect of keeping lay people quite separate from and subordinate to clergy. The Church was conceived in institutional and hierarchical terms: it was like an army with the clergy as the officer class. The clergy were powerful because God's grace was mediated through the sacraments only priests could administer. Lay members had a largely passive role as the recipients of clerical ministrations on the one hand, and as assistants to the clergy on the other. A. M. Fairbairn, a Congregationalist, pointed out that the effect of Anglo-Catholicism was to emphasize those aspects of Anglicanism that most marked it off from other Protestant churches:

> And so [the Church's] authority was magnified, the apostolicity of its orders and doctrines was affirmed, its bishops were invested with a more awful dignity, and its priests with more sacred functions; its Prayer-book was filled with a deeper significance, its services were made to articulate a larger and lovelier faith.[27]

The tendency to elevate the clerical office was considerably reinforced by what was frankly a cult of personality in the movement. All priests were revered as priests, but in addition some were held in awe because of their particular personality. These priests had hagiographies written about them. Some, like Bishop Edward King, were declared saints in their own lifetime or had monuments erected to them after their death; Newman gathered around him a group of young men who were so devoted to him that they even imitated his mannerisms and gestures.[28] It is not surprising that many catholic priests were at best paternalistic and at worst authoritarian and self-indulgent.

Second, this model did not encourage the clergy to think of ministry in collaborative terms. Ministry was what they alone did – the real work of the Church – for which they had received a special call by God. Father Mackonochie at St Alban's Holborn even found reading in church by lay people to be 'repugnant'.[29] We have already seen how such an understanding exacerbated tendencies to eccentricity. It tended to produce an isolated and lonely priesthood – something that the Anglo-Catholics saw not as a weakness but as a price priests had to be prepared to pay. It was also a model of ministry that was best suited to celibate priests or priests with a team of curates. Neither of these were realistic options for the majority of parishes in the second half of the twentieth century.

But the most unfortunate legacy of the movement has been its patriarchy and misogyny, thinly disguised as principled opposition to women priests. No church can preach equality or human rights to the secular world if it cannot set its own house in order first. The Church is paying a heavy price for this in the twenty-first century as generations of younger women (and men) detect the underlying attitude and stay away. This leaves the catholic tradition weak and inward-looking, more concerned with maintenance than mission.[30]

Conclusion

The memory of the catholic model lingers on and lies deep in the Anglican subconscious. In the absence of any other persuasive qualifying models it may yet exercise a powerful if unacknowledged influence among the non-evangelical clergy. This shows itself in two principal ways: the difficulty many clergy still have in being collaborative or even collegiate in their ministries; and their feelings of unfocused guilt when they are not being busy! For the more conservative, there are also issues about fully accepting women's ministry – as priests and bishops – that look simply bigoted in a society where sexual equality is not just taken for granted but regarded as a fundamental principle of morality. When Western democracies are telling the Muslim world to reform its treatment of women in the name of universal human rights, and when Muslim women see the advent of the modern state as their best hope, there is something perverse about the inability of male Christian clergy to see what is at stake in their continuing insistence on a male priesthood. The inclusive priesthood is one way in which God is made possible for a very sizeable part of the human community.

Curiously, however, what many clergy have lost from the catholic paradigm of ordained ministry is what lay at its very heart: the desire to save souls and make people holy within the Christian community of the Church of England and for the wider community.

If the witness of catholics is further diminished, what the Church of England as a whole may lose is its anchorage in that broader catholic tradition that understands that being a Christian is about being rooted in a historic community, a community that possesses the resources, accumulated over a long period of time, that are needed to go on nourishing the ethical, spiritual and liturgical life of people in changing times. And that would be a loss from which it might not recover.

6

Utility: the social activist
and personal therapist

Tell any Anglican priest in any part of the world that he is
no prophet and he will cheerfully agree that this is indeed so.
Tell him he has no gifts of leadership and while he may not like
it he will not greatly resent it. But tell him that he has no pastoral
sense and he will be really hurt, and feel deeply wounded and
insulted in the house of his friends.

Roger Lloyd

Obviously, if we all decided to accept and value ourselves, we would
cause those who have power over us a great deal of trouble.

Dorothy Rowe

Origins and evolution

Anglo-Catholic theology and understanding of ordained ministry
inspired growing numbers of clergy throughout the first half of the
twentieth century. This is not to say that a majority of clergy became
Anglo-Catholic; they did not. But they were encouraged by a relatively coherent theology of ministry and an example of hard-working,
self-confident and enthusiastic practice. In particular, the theology of
the *liberal* catholics came to the fore and, as the century progressed,
had an increasing influence on theology more widely. The aim of the
liberal catholics was to restate traditional doctrines in the light of
modern knowledge. But their doctrinal starting point was somewhat
different from that of the evangelicals, and in one respect it led to the
development of a type of social theology that was also to become
highly influential. By the mid-1960s, forms of liberal theology were
dominant in the universities, while many parish priests in urban and
industrial centres looked to social catholicism to supply workable
models of ordained ministry.

The liberal catholics made their mark with a series of books, beginning in 1889 with the publication of *Lux Mundi*.[1] This was subtitled

A Series of Studies in the Religion of the Incarnation. The focus on the incarnation as the key Christian doctrine meant that liberal catholic theology began with an affirmation of humanity (in that God had become human) and a relatively optimistic view of human possibility. The evangelicals tended to start with the Fall and original sin. But as catholic theologians reflected on society they also acknowledged how the moral and spiritual direction of many people's lives was influenced as much by their social circumstances as by acts of individual will. While an individual might seek to live a life of moral integrity, he or she was always caught up in the corporate life of institutions that operated according to a more selfish or self-regarding code. We would talk now about 'structural', 'systemic', 'institutional' or 'corporate' sin.[2] In bringing about change in the lives of individuals, the importance of changing the context in which they lived out their lives could not be ignored. A form of *social* as well as liberal catholicism developed that emphasized the need to move society as much as the individual in the direction of the kingdom of God.

In addition, the Church was understood as an extension of the incarnation, and so the instrument through which God continued to show his concern for and be involved in every aspect of human life and its redemption. It is not surprising, therefore, to find essays in *Lux Mundi* on such topics as ethics and politics, and to discover that Francis Paget's essay, 'Sacraments', emphasized their social aspect. Nor is it surprising to discover that many turned to socialist economic and social analyses as they sought to understand aspects of life in industrial Britain. Shaped by this incarnational theology the Church of England was able to bring a prophetic edge as well as a pastoral concern to its championing of those who worked in the sweat shops and lived in the slums. Church leaders like Charles Gore, the first Bishop of Birmingham, saw Christian socialism as the logical outcome of the religion of the incarnation. In this, many would follow.

In the second half of the twentieth century, this social catholicism continued to guide the pastoral ministries of Anglican clergy, reaching its high point in 1985 with the publication of *Faith in the City*, a report into the growing deprivation and neglect of England's urban priority areas.[3] During this period, many catholic clergy, battered by an aggressive, secular philosophy – logical positivism – found themselves holding less and less to catholic dogmas in the traditional sense. They did, however, remain wedded to catholic liturgical practices while finding that the social commitment of incarnational theology stimulated them into rethinking what being a pastor might mean in a society that was abandoning churchgoing and turning to the secular pastors of the burgeoning welfare state. Before we consider these new directions for ministry, however, we need to recall something of the Anglican commitment to pastoral ministry.

The socially useful pastor

In the Church of England's ordination service, the bishop declares that the priest must 'set the Good Shepherd always before him as the pattern of his calling'.[4] Pastoral work has been distinctive of Anglican ministry since the Reformation, even if it has not always been conscientiously undertaken. For many clergy, pastoral concern remains the heart of ordained ministry.

One of the principal aims of the reformers was to make pastoring central to the work of the priest once more. In the medieval Church, clergy were involved in a wide variety of activities as one of the few educated groups in society. Apart from saying mass, their work might be wholly secular: they might be in the service of kings or aristocrats as secretaries, clerks, administrators and private chaplains, or teachers and mentors for their children. The reformers wanted the clergy to be pastors to their flocks. For the first four hundred years of Anglican history this was relatively unproblematic. England was a Christian country and the Church of England was the established Church, organized on a paro-chial basis. As we have already seen, the parson was a recognized figure in the community whose pastoral ministry was unquestioned. He did not have to make too careful a distinction between those who were regular attenders at his church and those who were parishioners in a wider sense; all were his pastoral responsibility and he sought to minister to them all. This is not to deny those times and circumstances in Anglican history in which clergy failed to live up to this pastoral ideal. When clergy were not resident, pastoral care might be minimal – little more than the maintenance of Sunday services and the occasional offices by unbeneficed clergy. Equally unsatisfactory was the widespread practice of clergy acting as law enforcement officers in the eighteenth and early nineteenth centuries. It required a considerable act of imagination to accept that the clerical magistrate who was sending you to the stocks or to gaol was exercising pastoral care on your behalf.[5] Despite this, English people came, on the whole, to value the pastoral care that the parson showed towards the people of his parish, whether they came to church or not, and the renewal of pastoral ministry was an important feature of both the catholic and evangelical revivals in the Church of England. Even as churchgoing declined during the course of the twentieth century, and the clergyman's religious services were required less and less, his pastoral ministry was, for the first half of the century at any rate, still valued: the parson was socially useful because he had a pastoral role.

Clerical handbooks from this period – such as Peter Green's *The Town Parson*, published in 1919 – set considerable store by pastoral work whose effectiveness, it was generally believed, was the result of first-hand knowledge of people gained through extensive visiting. Green wrote:

> The most regular, careful, and beautiful services, the most eloquent and thoughtful preaching, the most elaborate music, not one or all of these things will supply the lack of that true pastoral relationship which nothing but personal knowledge of your people will give. I am convinced that the old saying, 'A house-going parson makes a church-going people' is true.[6]

Green was following in the tradition that dated back to George Herbert's *The Country Parson* (1633). Herbert had recommended the systematic visiting of the parish by quarters.[7] As town parishes increased in size and the numbers of parochial clergy began to fall, this seemed like an increasingly tall order, and may be one reason why Green thought a day off could not really be justified for men over 40![8] At any rate, most Anglican clergy came to accept that house visiting was an important part of their duties, and the English people came to expect it.

The loss of social usefulness

But after the Second World War, the social position of the clergy changed significantly. First, the value of their religious expertise was called into question. By then, religion had become the concern of a diminishing number of people, as the figures for Easter communicants in the Church of England show. At first glance the true picture is somewhat obscured by a rise in numbers in the early part and the midpoint of the century. In the first two decades, for example, numbers increased, reaching a peak of 2,390,000 in 1927; thereafter, however, they fell steadily year by year until the late 1940s, when there was a revival. A new peak of 2,167,000 communicants was reached in 1956, but thereafter the decline continued at the pre-war rate. In fact, these two small peaks mask a longer overall decline, beginning in the 1880s, which is clearly discerned if we take the longer view. But whatever our starting point, the collapse in church attendance in the post-war period cannot be denied, even if it cannot be wholly explained.[9]

At the same time as church attendance fell, people's understanding of what religion was changed: the assumption that religion and Christianity were synonymous was increasingly challenged. Inward migration brought large numbers of adherents of other world faiths to Britain and the New Age movement offered people a range of alternative spiritualities that did not need the Church or the clergy at all: religion was deregulated and privatized, set adrift from its previous mooring in faith communities.[10]

Anglican clergy were disappointed with these trends but by no means disheartened. Even if their more priestly role was only valued by a diminishing minority, their pastoral role remained and was universally welcomed. Or so they believed. However, the creation and expansion of the welfare state after 1945 led to the growth of a range of professionals, particularly in the social services, whose various specialisms seemed to cut the ground from under the feet of the Christian pastor. In the years after 1945 people in need of pastoral help learnt to turn first to the social and welfare workers and last, if at all, to the clergy. Clergy came to be seen as well-meaning amateurs in a world of professional carers. Moreover, many felt, rightly or wrongly, that clerical pastoring came at a price they were not prepared to pay: clergy wanted your soul.

In a post-Christian culture with a developed system of professional care, the pastoral role of Christian clergy beyond their own faith communities is likely to remain problematic. While individual clergy and social workers may get to know and respect one another and find ways of working together in particular local situations, tensions between the two occupational groups are never far away and can easily surface. Those who trained as social workers have been thoroughly grounded in secular disciplines and may be wary of those who, it could be thought, might have an ulterior motive. I witnessed this at first-hand in 1989 when there was an emergency at the Hillsborough football ground in Sheffield. A surge in the crowd had resulted in many young men being hurt, some crushed to death. Local radio appealed for clergy and social workers to go to the ground to help – and many did. Yet despite the best efforts of senior workers in both professions, many social workers viewed the arrival of clergy with intense suspicion if not hostility, being unsure about their motives and competencies alike.[11]

All people like to think that the jobs they do are valued by the wider community. The ordained minister is no exception. The calling into question of the clergy's social usefulness as pastor as well as priest dealt the morale of Anglican clergy an almost lethal blow. As the social usefulness of the clergy became a matter of contention within the wider community, some clergy sought to resolve the difficulties they experienced by unconsciously (or consciously) assimilating the pastoral role of ordained ministry to various secular models of pastoral care that they believed to be more acceptable in a more secular culture. A few clergy based almost their whole ministry on such models (especially during the period from the late 1960s to the 1990s) but all clergy were (and remain) open to being influenced by them and the human sciences (with their secular assumptions) on which they draw. Two models of pastoral care have been of particular importance during this time. I will call these 'the pastor as community activist'[12] and 'the pastor as personal therapist'.

I will first describe each approach and then offer some critical comments, trying to see what insights are of value for ministry and where particular dangers lie for the Church and its mission and ministry if models are accepted too uncritically.

The model: social activist

Origins

From the late 1960s, as its religious influence waned, the Church of England became increasingly interested in political issues, if not actually politicized. There were various reasons for this, not least a growing uncertainty among younger clergy about the morality of devoting too much time and energy to specifically religious activities when issues of life and death on planet earth seemed very pressing. We were living through a time when the threat of nuclear annihilation was very real, when doubts about the capacity of the welfare state to eliminate poverty were beginning to surface and when the reality of world poverty and hunger was brought home most forcefully in hard-hitting news reports and documentaries on television. At the same time, theology itself turned its attention to the secular world and declared secularization to be not the enemy of the gospel but part of God's plan for the world.[13] A spate of books appeared on the need for the Church to speak to secularized men and women in secular fashion. The half-formed thoughts about religionless Christianity in Dietrich Bonhoeffer's *Letters and Papers from Prison* and the secular gospels of Paul van Buren and Bishop John Robinson were quoted with enthusiasm.[14] For a while at least the language of theology became decidedly political and decidedly left-wing, while the most overworked biblical text became: 'let justice roll down like waters, and righteousness like an ever-flowing stream'.[15] This activity intensified sharply after 1979, when the country elected a Conservative government with, under Margaret Thatcher, a radical programme of reforms that put it at odds with all those – and this included by then many if not most of the clergy – who believed that the economic and social ills of the nation required more public spending and government intervention. But how could this be paid for? The answer was clear: by abandoning the hugely costly nuclear deterrent. Unilateral nuclear disarmament achieved the twin objectives of freeing up money for welfare programmes and moving the nation towards a more Christian position on war, for few believed that the use of nuclear weapons was compatible with the Christian theory of just war. The agendas of synods and church councils began to reflect these concerns. So, for example, in an attempt to influence the policy of national government, a report was produced for the General

Synod that recommended the unilateral abandonment of nuclear weapons (though Synod did not endorse it). This was the only area of policy where the Church wanted less spending and not more!

From the mid-1960s, under the impact – albeit indirect – of Liberation Theology, some clergy began to speak of God's particular concern for or bias towards the poor.[16] If God had such a bias, the Church ought to have the same bias. This led in the larger towns to some clergy taking an active part in city politics and, following the urban riots of 1981, to the Archbishop of Canterbury commissioning a report, *Faith in the City*, which was highly critical of the policies of (mainly) Conservative government in urban priority areas.[17] The Church was politicized in the sense both that political concerns became a prominent part of its agenda and that there was a tendency on the part of a growing number of people to believe that theology and the Bible could yield direct answers to complex economic and political questions. (It did not escape the notice of some commentators at the time that while the Church of England seemed incapable of offering advice on what most people regarded as fairly straightforward moral issues, such as abortion or homosexuality, it did not hesitate to condemn various pieces of government legislation, such as the poll tax, as 'unbiblical' or 'immoral'.) By 1988 a contributor to *The Spectator* felt able to begin an article by saying:

> There was a time when the denunciation of a major government policy by the Church of England would have sent shockwaves rippling through the political consciousness of the nation. Nowadays these things happen as a matter of course ...[18]

The practice of community activism

In such a climate it was not surprising to find that some clergy, particularly though not exclusively in urban areas, came to practise a pastoral ministry that was a form of community activism or community work.[19] This was not social work – the brief temptation of an earlier generation – for the community activist was not so much concerned with the problems of individuals and their families as with those 'structures' that were held to be responsible for their plight. Whereas a social worker might seek to help a poor family sort out welfare entitlements when the council increased rents, the community activist would be helping the local tenants' federation to raise consciousness about the issue on the housing estates and organize a march to the town hall to get the policy reversed. This was pastoral ministry with a prophetic edge. Needless to say, the traditional pastoral response of offering the poor relief through charity was thoroughly despised: this more politicized Church preferred the language of social justice to the language of charity. People should have their 'rights', not charity; and those who objected to this approach were vilified as political and theological reactionaries.

This model of pastoral ministry was sometimes given theological underpinning by forms of British Liberation Theology.[20] Although Liberation Theologies began in places where poverty was far more severe than anything experienced in contemporary Britain, they had a consid-erable if indirect influence on a younger generation of clergy who saw their own ministries (especially in places of urban or rural poverty) as equally concerned with liberating the poor from unjust and oppressive structures. The language of social justice was assimilated so successfully into the Christian vocabulary at this time that many people have prob-ably come to think that it is biblical.

The start of my own ministry coincides with this period, and as I look back I can see that it fell exactly into this pattern. I became a parish priest in inner-city Sheffield in 1972 at the age of 30, just as the city was beginning to be convulsed by major economic change. The steel, cutlery and coal-mining industries in which my parishioners worked were all facing a slow collapse. Within a few years a substantial propor-tion of the men of working age in the parish were out of work. Families were becoming poorer. At the same time, the quality of public services was beginning to run down, including housing, education and medical care. Raising the consciousness of my congregation to the unjust social and economic structures of contemporary British society became an important part of ministry. I came to the view that the best way I could help my parishioners was by setting up a community project to help them improve the quality of their life together – through the provision of a children's playground, an advice centre and community social activities. When the bishop offered me a curate I chose to have a community worker instead. After a time, I also came to the conclusion that rather than suffer the poor decision-making of the local council, I would offer myself as a candidate for public office – and became an elected member for 13 years. In all these ways I was not at all unusual for the times.

The model in practice

A critique of the pastor as social activist

What is the value of this approach and what are the dangers? Perhaps the major gain was that it enabled some clergy to find a way into the life of their local communities that they had not found before, and to bring the concerns of those communities into the prayer of the Church. Some individual clergy (not necessarily clergy in general) began to gain some respect from the secular pastors – the social, community and welfare workers. But this was often done at a cost, and on balance I suspect that the gains were considerably outweighed by the losses.

What of the dangers? First, the rationale for this approach was really based on a series of non sequiturs of the kind: God has a concern for everything including politics, therefore the organized Church ought to have a concern for everything including politics; the Bible is about God, who knows about everything including politics, therefore by going to the Bible we can find answers to everything including politics. This led to some very simplistic attempts to read off from the Bible simple solutions to complex economic and social issues. But the truth is that while God has a concern for everything, the task he has committed to his Church is more limited: it is to make God possible by announcing the good news of Jesus Christ and nourishing faith in him. Likewise, while God knows everything, the Bible does not contain everything that God knows. The Bible is principally concerned with *saving* knowledge; if we want to know how to run an economy or a housing policy we have to resort to appropriate sources of secular knowledge and wisdom. Clergy, therefore, need to be very cautious about offering opinions on matters where their theoretical knowledge or practical knowledge is no greater than any other informed member of the public and a great deal less than any experts in the field. Clergy need to know they are truly lay people in these matters.[21]

Second, the assimilation of ordained ministry to models of community activism meant that some clergy never considered it appropriate to commend the Christian gospel too energetically in case this compromised their neutrality in the eyes of the community. The task of evangelism was neglected and sometimes repudiated altogether. The only form of witness that was really possible was the witness of altruistic involvement in community affairs. Some clergy were in any case uncomfortable in their more 'religious' roles: they resented the amount of time, energy and money that went into supporting buildings used exclusively for worship; they accepted the criticism of religion as being overly concerned with 'pie in the sky when you die'; they wanted to give people pie now. So they turned worship itself into a consciousness-raising exercise for the church membership, who generally regarded the political agendas of their priest as out of place in sacred liturgy. Clergy working to a community-activist model frequently failed to carry the local church with them. We may never know how many people slipped away and were lost to the Church during this period.

In the third place, clergy influenced by this paradigm of pastoral ministry simply failed to appreciate how the gospel itself liberates people in a way that nothing else can. The gospel presupposition is that we have no power of ourselves to help ourselves, but once we open ourselves to the power of the Holy Spirit working in us then all things are possible. People are prevented from improving their own lot and that of their communities by many things, but above all by their own lack of confidence and feeling of worth. The gospel call to embrace Jesus Christ as Lord empowers individuals by freeing them from their past, affirming their worth and value as those for whom Christ died, and promising them the help of the Holy Spirit in transforming their lives. Where people accept such a gospel (as we see from the early history of Methodism, nineteenth-century evangelicalism and Anglo-Catholicism, and contemporary worldwide Pentecostalism), individual lives are changed: people become more confident individuals, they change their personal behaviour, becoming more caring spouses, more loving parents, more industrious workers and more honest neighbours.[22] Rippling out from this, the lives of communities and ultimately nations are changed as well. In short, people who experience the power of the gospel become agents again and are not simply victims. Clergy who have not experienced such power at work in their own lives are destined to seek substitutes and dress them up as the gospel. But for the poor who have responded to this gospel, it is political action and the promises of politicians that look like pie in the sky: the Holy Spirit transforms lives in the here and now.

The final criticism of the community-activist approach is that in drawing on Liberation Theologies it was based on a raft of not always acknowledged political assumptions of a socialist sort, summarized in the idea of social justice. This is made very clear in Laurie Green's manual for those who want to practise a community-activist model of pastoral ministry, *Let's Do Theology*. Green emphasizes that we can only 'do theology' if we already have a 'deep commitment to transformation' – the starting point of all Liberation Theologies.[23] However, the sort of social transformation Green has in mind is not any kind of social change but the transformation of society in a socialist or at least anti-capitalist direction. This is why proponents of this type of theologizing are scornful of the idea of charity or philanthropy as the Christian's response to the poor. What community activists want is not the limited redistribution of resources that comes from the generosity of wealthier individuals, but the far more radical and comprehensive redistribution that only the state can bring about. But if there is to be a redistribution of resources in society through politics rather than philanthropy – if, in other words, some of the assets of one group of people are to be seized by the state and transferred to another – the language of social justice has to be invoked. The state needs to be able to justify what it is doing in moral terms, otherwise – to rephrase Proudhon – socialism is theft.[24]

It is sometimes argued that the Bible – in particular the Old Testament prophets – demands 'social justice'. It is true that the Bible recognizes that the world is marked by inequalities between people and speaks of our moral and religious duty to act righteously by showing compassion towards those less fortunate than ourselves. But the demand for compassion to the poor was not based on the belief that all inequality was the result of injustice: it did not assume that the poor had a right to the wealth of others. How could it, since poverty and suffering are the result of a variety of factors, not only injustice and oppression but also failed harvests and a lack of natural resources, incompetence and idleness – as the Bible knows well. The Bible demanded righteousness – treating people fairly, not exploiting the poor, showing compassion and generosity towards the weak – not social justice in the modern sense of distributive justice. But socialism needs the language of social justice since its programme is one of compulsory redistribution through taxation. To take resources from one group of people and give them to another will feel like robbery unless it can be shown to be a matter of justice. Those who adopted a community-activist role during the 1970s and 1980s and got into the way of using the language of social justice, reinforced by the language of rights, assumed this was what the prophets were talking about, and poured scorn on the biblical idea of charity and philanthropy.

This exaltation of social justice and denigration of charity has been unfortunate, perhaps even unforgivable. On the one hand, by encouraging people in need to seek 'justice' (the complete removal of inequality) rather than help, we make it difficult for them to accept solutions that are improvements but not necessarily perfect solutions. The needy then live out their lives in a state of permanent discontent. On the other hand, by insisting that only justice will do, we discourage those who want to respond to those in need but fear their small actions will not be welcomed because they are insufficient to meet the demand for justice. We then gradually kill off the altruism of the better off. These difficulties are removed if Christian pastors and the Christian Church learn again the biblical language of charity rather than the political rhetoric of social justice, and encourage people to respond to those needs of others that they can do something about.[25]

But for much of the period from the 1970s onwards, the language of social justice and rights became part of the stock-in-trade of many clergy who adopted a community-activist approach to pastoral ministry (and through them church councils and synods). For such clergy, anxious to improve their pastoral – that is, community-activist – skills, it became fashionable to use their sabbaticals to make secular pilgrimages across the Atlantic to learn the techniques of 'community organizing' in Chicago – where President Barack Obama was to work as a community activist – or to read the Bible politically in Peru. However, the collapse of socialist economies in eastern Europe, the abandonment of socialism by New

Labour in Britain, the embracing of capitalism by China and the cooling of enthusiasm for socialist solutions even on the part of some Latin American Liberation Theologians, has effectively put a question mark against some of the theoretical foundations of this whole approach, and caused practitioners to think again about the basis of their ministry.

There are also theological grounds for questioning the adequacy of the concept of social justice. The gospel is, after all, not about the strict application of justice but about God's generosity. If we were to be treated according to our just deserts our position before God would be hopeless. But God acts towards us out of love and with generosity, not according to our merit or desert. This is the point of such parables as the Prodigal Son and the Labourers in the Vineyard. Similarly, there are many in society who scarcely merit help, who would not qualify if we applied the test of justice, but who nevertheless need it: the recidivist criminal, the persistent alcoholic, the child molester, the habitual drug user. Their only hope is that others act towards them with charity and not strict justice.

It is possible that after the collapse of the financial and banking system from late 2008, and the rise in the national debt to quite staggering proportions, in the coming decades the welfare state will be progressively dismantled or seriously eroded or radically transformed. There will no doubt be casualities. It would be a tragedy if Christians felt inhibited from acting with charity on the grounds that they could not secure complete justice.

The model: personal therapist

The influence of the counselling movement

During the 1980s, as left-wing politics went into the doldrums and only emerged when it became right-wing politics (New Labour), the general climate became less political and more therapeutic. In other words, people became more concerned with their own personal emotional well-being than with changing society.[26] Some clergy now began to redefine the pastoral task, moving away from a concern for structures and back to a concern for individual people. They had noted the growth of the counselling and psychotherapy movement and sought to use the theory and practice of so-called non-directive counselling in their own pastoral ministries. In this way they believed they could find a new relevance for the pastoral ministry. The approach was given a considerable boost by the publication of Alastair Campbell's book, *Rediscovering Pastoral Care* – a book that has been widely used by both ministers and those training for ordained ministry since it was first published in 1981.[27]

Campbell claimed that the book was an attempt to recover traditional understandings of pastoral care – hence the title. But although he makes reference to classic Christian texts, it is very much a passing reference. He is not so much influenced by the Christian tradition of pastoral care as by contemporary counselling theory, in particular that of the American psychologist Carl Rogers. He is not alone in drawing inspiration from this source. The Rogerian approach has come to dominate pastoral theology and practice both in the United States and Britain. Howard Clinebell, an American pastoral theologian also influenced by Rogers, has summarized the principal aim of the approach in this way:

> Facilitating the maximum development of a person's potentialities, at each stage of life, in ways that contribute to the growth of others as well and to the development of a society in which all persons will have an opportunity to use their full potentialities . . .[28]

Writing under the influence of this tradition, Campbell makes two major points about the nature of pastoring. First, he insists that pastoring cannot be confined to the clergy. He says this because he accepts at face value Rogers' insistence that what makes for successful counselling is not knowledge or expertise but the quality of the relationship between counsellor and client:

> It has gradually been driven home to me that I cannot help . . . by means of any intellectual or training procedure. No approach which relies upon knowledge, upon training, upon acceptance of something that is *taught*, is of any use . . . The failure of any such approach through the intellect had forced me to recognize that change appears to come about through experience in a relationship.[29]

This leads Campbell to the not unreasonable conclusion that anyone may offer pastoral care since it is the ability to create a relationship, not the possession of knowledge or the acquiring of expertise, that makes for successful pastoring.

In the second place, Campbell believes that what makes for successful counselling is the common humanity of the carer and the other. 'Pastoral care is grounded', he argues, 'in mutuality, not in expertise; it is possible because we share a common humanity with all the splendour and all the fallibility which that implies.'[30] Carers can offer help because they have known for themselves similar emotional and other problems. However, he is also clear that creating a warm relationship, though necessary, is not sufficient for pastoral care to be given. Pastors must also exhibit a further quality that Campbell calls 'personal integrity'. By integrity he appears to mean having a certain cluster of personal qualities, the most important of which is an 'outward honesty' that reflects an 'inner steadfastness', such that one can speak of the 'wholeness and oneness' of a person. This integrated personality can then face any situation without fear. Joan of Arc, as portrayed by George Bernard Shaw, is cited by Campbell as an example of someone with this personal integrity. At her trial, Joan finally cannot deny the truth of her voices any longer, even though telling the truth will result in her being burnt. Her integrity, which comes from 'loyalty to an inner truth', results in absolute fearlessness. How she behaves and what she says (her outward honesty) is now at one with what she believes and feels (her inner steadfastness). It is this quality of personal integrity which, for Campbell, must lie at the heart of the offer of pastoral care.

In some respects the example of Joan of Arc is a strange one. That kind of integrity – an integrity bordering on fanaticism – would not, on the face of it, seem to be the first quality one would look for in a pastor, though in fairness we have already noted that Campbell also speaks of the need for pastors to be warm, understanding and sincere – not all of which are the qualities that spring to mind when one thinks of the Maid of Orleans. What pastors do is to offer to the person in need their own integrity, hammered out on the anvil of their own human experience. He writes:

> If I can find some courage, hope and transcendence in the midst of life, then I can help my fellow men find that same wholeness; for I know that I am no better than they, no wiser, no more deserving of such fulfilment.[31]

This sentiment seems to be echoed and amplified by Jeffrey Masson writing as an eight-year, Freudian-trained psychotherapist who came to think that what he offered was of little worth most of the time and little better than people receive from family or friends:

> At times I could offer no genuine assistance, yet rarely did I acknowledge this to the patient. My life was in no better shape than that of my patients. Any advice I might have had to offer would be no better than that of a well-informed friend (and considerably more expensive). I must assume that none of this was unique to me.[32]

The model in practice

A critique of the pastor as personal therapist

On the face of it, Campbell's aim – to offer others something of the pastor's own integrity or experience – seems laudable as far as it goes; but it does not go very far. Pastors can learn from the counselling movement the need to be warm and empathetic and people of integrity. But none of this offers guidance to pastors as to what they should say or do in any given situation. This is because Campbell defines pastoral care in a way that focuses not on the content of what might be said but only on what is needed to establish rapport. It is not particularly or distinctively Christian. One could hold any religious views or none and still offer this kind of care to one's neighbour. The approach rests on the assumption that what we need to know in order to offer pastoral care can be known without particular reference to the Christian tradition: it is knowledge that can be found by anyone from within their own experience. Indeed, as we have already noted, under the influence of Carl Rogers, Campbell repudiates the very idea that pastoral care could require 'expertise of any kind'. He sums up his position by saying that 'in describing pastoral care we are speaking of the mediation of steadfastness and wholeness, not the offering of advice at an intellectual level, nor the eliciting of insight at an emotional level'.[33] When, therefore, he refers to the Bible and Christian history in the rest of his book, he is simply using people and images from the Christian tradition – the wounded healer, the fool – as examples or illustrations of these human qualities of steadfastness, wholeness and caring: he is not suggesting that there is vital knowledge to be had there and perhaps nowhere else.

But this will not do. In the first place, it will not do as an account of what pastoral care in general might be. It assumes that all human beings draw the right (and the same) conclusions from reflecting on their experience, so that what they offer in caring for another turns out to be helpful and not destructive. But different people draw different and even contradictory conclusions as they reflect on their lives; not every reflection on experience is equally helpful – or equally true – simply because it is drawn directly from one's own experience. Some people who have wrestled with issues for themselves and exhibit great personal integrity nevertheless make very poor pastoral judgements. Integrity by itself guarantees nothing.

Nor will it do in the second place as an account of what makes for specifically Christian pastoral care: for care to be Christian, to some extent at least, it would have to draw from and depend on the Christian tradition, on the Christian understanding of God, his nature, purposes and relationship to the world, and the Christian understanding of people – their nature and destiny. No one can offer Christian pastoral care without at least some knowledge of the Christian tradition – and that implies a kind of expertise, something Campbell explicitly denies. It is not, of course, the kind of expertise the person in the pew is incapable of acquiring. Quite the contrary, for all Christians are expected to grow in the knowledge of God through prayer, through receiving the sacrament, through studying God's word in Scripture and through the fellowship of the Church. The trouble with Campbell's account of pastoral care is that it encourages people to be impatient with the Bible and Christian doctrine and the discipline needed to assimilate them. The Rogerian counselling model that lies behind what Campbell writes at every point is superficially attractive: it suggests that the key to success-ful pastoring lies in securing a certain attitude and approach rather than being steeped in the Christian story. It has little to do with the tradition of Christian pastoral care. I would certainly want to argue that Christian pastoral care cannot be confined to the ordained ministry, though not for the reason Campbell advances here. Nevertheless, I also believe that the clergy have particular pastoral responsibilities that depend on their acquiring knowledge of the Christian tradition, and skills in communicating it and bringing it to bear in the life of individuals and communities.

The concept of non-directive counselling

At the heart of secular counselling is the commitment to a non-judgemental and non-directive approach. I have doubts about whether any counselling could be non-directive: counsellors must have some idea as to whether their client is making progress (that is, moving in the right direction) or not. If not, keeping clients in therapy or sending them on their way seems a most arbitrary decision. Christian pastors must cer-tainly have some idea of what progress would be. Similarly I suspect that the claim of counsellors to be non-judgemental is somewhat disingenu-ous: would a counsellor really make no judgement about the behaviour of a self-confessed child molester? What counsellors often mean when they say they are 'non-judgemental' is that for all practical purposes they fall back on what they think is uncontroversial – usually some kind of utilitarian ethic, where the test of any action is whether it leads to an increase in human happiness, particularly the happiness of the client. But Christians could not accept such an ethic: the question for Christians is not whether there is some course of action that leads to greater happiness but whether it is what God wants. There may be times when what God wants may not make people happy – at least not in the short term – because it conflicts with their own desires. As we move deeper into a post-Christian age, the differences between Christians and non-Christians on a whole range of ethical issues are becoming more apparent. While the Christian constituency itself does not speak with one voice, there are distinctive Christian voices to be heard – especially among the laity – on such matters as euthanasia, abortion, sex outside marriage and homosexuality. The temptation for Christian pastors influenced by the counselling movement is that they confuse the utilitarian ethic with Christian compassion.

But the ordained pastor has an important role, which is to help Christians see how the Christian faith bears on pastoral situations. This has been called an 'interpretive style' of ministry.[34]

Strengths and weaknesses

The two popular models of pastoral care that have influenced so much clergy practice since the 1960s are both, then, seriously flawed. This is not to say that there are no useful techniques that can be learnt from them – as long as we keep our critical faculties on full alert. But they are not paradigms for Christian pastors. If we want to move on from here, we need to begin again by re-examining the Christian pastoral tradition.

When we turn to that tradition, not to raid it for illustrations but to let it challenge our present practice, we find that we are in a different world from the one described by Alastair Campbell. If, for example, we look at the pastoral handbooks of George Herbert and Richard Baxter, which have been read by the clergy in every period of Anglican history until the last 40 or so years, what both men regarded as quite central to their work as pastors was the *spiritual* health of the people committed to their charge. They would offer material help and emotional support to individuals and families when appropriate, but this was no more than any other Christian would offer to his or her neighbour; it was not distinctive of the ordained ministry. The pastor's task was to prepare souls for heaven, to help – in Herbert's words – shrivelled hearts recover greenness. At some point in the Church's more recent history, this emphasis changed: the cure of souls ceased to be central, and concern for people's emotional and material well-being assumed priority.

Conclusion

The social activists have taught us that pastoring cannot be the task of the clergy alone. If Christian care is to be offered effectively in a community, it must be done by every member of the local church. Each individual Christian is a pastor to his fellow Christians and to his neighbour. The congregation is a therapeutic community where individuals can find acceptance and love but also standards and benchmarks. The clergy have a responsibility to build up a pastorally minded and pastorally effective group of people. This does not mean that apart from this building up, the pastoral role of the clergy is no different from that of other members of the church. On the contrary, the clergy will still be looked to as an important pastoral resource by the lay members of a local church. The clergy get to know particularly well certain members of the church – the church council and officers, the leaders of organizations. To a considerable extent they may well become *pastor pastorum* in their local church. This will partly come with the appointment and partly depend on the way each individual ordained minister exercises his or her ministry. But in addition, clergy have a two-fold representative function. First, they represent the local Christian church to the wider community: when they visit the sick, for example, they do so unambiguously on behalf of and in the name of the congregation as a whole. This is why there is more than a grain of truth in people saying the church did not visit them even though a lay member of the congregation did. They are not saying they were not visited by a member of the local church, but that they were not visited in this 'representative' way. Second, clergy are charged with bringing people face to face with God as they break the bread and break open the word week by week. They make God possible.

We might finally reflect on the great events of late 2008–9: the global credit crisis. A generation of younger adults who had only ever known prosperity and rising living standards were suddenly faced with the possibility that this could all be snatched away in a moment. The crisis affected people differently. Some lost their jobs and homes, others their savings. Most did not. But everyone grew fearful. It was a sharp reminder of the sheer contingency of human life. It caused people to reassess. What was important? What was life about? Where was God to be found? These were important spiritual questions, aspects of what we have called in these chapters 'finding God'. Helping people at such moments to make sense of their lives – interpretive ministry – is the pastoral task. For to be ordained is to stand at the boundary between the mundane and the sacred; to bear witness to the transcendent; and to make God possible. Once that is forgotten, the pastoral vocation has been lost.

Part 3

FUTURE POSSIBILITIES

7

Making God possible in the twenty-first century

Artificial fertilizers make atheists.

Dutch proverb

They stand – these local heroes, these saints and sinners, these men and women of God – in that difficult space between the living and the dead, between faith and fear, between humanity and Christianity and say out loud, 'Behold I show you a mystery'.

Thomas Lynch

In this final chapter I want to focus on two aspects of contemporary Britain that, taken together, will point us towards the kind of ordained ministry the Church will need for the foreseeable future if it is to serve the mission of making God possible. This is not so much a radical change as a reordering of priorities in the way the clergy understand the nature of their task and the training that is appropriate to that. I will consider, first, the rise of secular humanism, which presents the Church with a serious challenge, and second, the persistence of the demand for the pastoral offices and occasional services, which presents it with serious encouragement. By reflecting on both we should be able to form a clearer idea of the way forward.

The encircling gloom

The last two decades or so have not been easy for religious believers. We are the first generations to enter what may come to be seen as the beginning of a post-Christian and perhaps post-religious era, at least as far as Europe is concerned. During this time, we have seen spectacular successes in science and technology. This has led many to think there is no intellectual problem that science cannot solve and no practical one that the application of science – technology – cannot fix. Whereas at one time the human race looked for certainty and control in magic, then in religion, then briefly in totalitarianisms (think of Lenin, Hitler and Mao), now it looks to science. There is no need either to postulate

God's existence or to summon his help – in which respect see the Dutch proverb quoted above. At the same time as science and technology have triumphed, religion has shown its darker side. There can be little doubt that the rise of religious fundamentalism – especially, though not exclusively, Islamic extremism – has done religion a great disservice among both the intellectual and opinion-forming elites, as well as the population more generally. According to a profile in the *New Yorker* in February 2009, for example, the British novelist Ian McEwan turned away from an interest in mysticism to 'science and rationality' following the issuing in 1989 of a fatwa by Ayatollah Khomeini against McEwan's friend and fellow writer, Salman Rushdie, and other subsequent Islamist outrages. He told his interviewer, 'The powers of sweet reason look a lot more attractive post 9/11 [than] the beckonings of faith, and I no longer put them in equal scales.'[1] Yet it is not so long ago that some of the country's leading intellectuals and people of letters were Christians and argued passionately for Christian belief – G. K. Chesterton, Dorothy L. Sayers, C. S. Lewis, T. S. Eliot. It is probably also true to say that many young people watching television programmes or reading articles in 2009 to mark the 150th anniversary of the publication of Charles Darwin's *On the Origin of Species* will have heard or read about how evolutionary science 'undermined' religious accounts of the creation and made God redundant. Some of those programmes and articles will have implied that Christian belief commits its contemporary followers to hold anti-evolutionary if not anti-scientific doctrines. Proof of this would come from the mouth of a certain sort of conservative American evangelical – properly called a 'fundamentalist' – always on hand to give the 'Christian' understanding of the origins of the world.[2] The views of scientists who were also believers would almost certainly not be sought. Then in Ireland and the United States, and now in Britain, stories about the predatory sexual behaviour of some Roman Catholic priests, and attempts by some in the hierarchy to cover it up, have played a similar role in causing many to question the institutional Church and its faith.[3] So the stories that have dominated the media have tended to erode rather than sustain Christianity for at least 25 years.

Yet what has been happening recently has only served to focus more sharply debates about religion that the British people have been having with themselves for a very long time. We have seen that for more than 50 years the British, along with other Europeans, have been walking away from the Christian churches and from organized religion. For a while, in Britain, people continued to have some grounding in the faith through the daily acts of worship and religious education of the school. This in turn might be reinforced through the media, especially the BBC. However, since the 1970s state schools have taught comparative religion rather than Christian faith, and the act of collective Christian worship has given way to a moralizing assembly. The religious output of the media has reduced throughout that time. This has produced a generation of young people who have been indifferent or even hostile towards Christianity, and not so much idealistic as moralistic.[4] (The question of where moral principles have come from is ignored, yet a moment's thought would make it clear that the morality of another religion – the Taleban version of Islam, for instance – or some secular philosophy – such as Nazism – would produce very different themes for assemblies. Christianity is not the only source of morality, but it has been the major influence: the values by which most people live are still recognizably Christian.) The enemies of religion, the committed and evangelistic atheists, have seized the moment, and while they are as yet a minority of the population, because they are disproportionately represented among the nation's opinion-formers they exercise an influence out of all proportion to their size. According to opinion polls, more and more people say they are atheists.[5]

The rise of secular humanism

Yet atheism is not a creed or a philosophy. It is, quite simply, a denial. It is parasitic on the religion it repudiates.[6] This was illustrated in 2009, when a few militant atheists in England who had been christened as infants demanded the right to be able to record their rejection of Christianity in the church's baptism registers. They are still living in a world where the rules are set by religion. Yet there is a sense in which we are all atheists in relation to some version of God. Socrates was accused of corrupting the youth of Athens and of atheism. Yet he was no non-believer: he simply did not believe in the gods of the city – a bad mistake since the city fathers took exception to that and put him to death. The first Christians were also accused of atheism, and did not deny it. Justin Martyr, early in the second century, confessed that Christians were atheists in that they denied the reality of all the gods worshipped in the Roman Empire with the exception of the 'most true God'.[7] Atheism as such does not bring some alternative set of coherent principles to guide thinking on the issues that life is constantly throwing at us. It is forms of secular humanism that do that. Humanism is a form of faith, and it is this the Christian minister needs to think about, since it is Christianity's faith-rival in contemporary Britain.

We should not measure the strength of humanism in the way the strength of Christianity is measured. Christianity submits to two tests: membership and answers to questionnaires that require respondents to choose between belief in God and non-belief. But a humanist does not have to join the British Humanist Association to be a humanist, nor does he or she have to deny God's existence, but only accept that God's existence is not proven. Many humanists simply want to leave the question of God to one side as speculative, unproductive and neither here nor there. The late Sir Bernard Crick, for example, a former president of the British Humanist Association, was very clear that he was not an atheist but a humanist.[8] On the question of God, he had nothing to say one way or another. He lacked evidence – though what 'evidence' would count *for* God's existence is not clear. In this respect, many humanists are to be distinguished from atheists such as Richard Dawkins and Christopher Hitchens, for whom lack of evidence is certain disproof of God's existence. (There are, of course, profound philosophical issues here around the idea of 'exists'. God does not 'exist' in the way tables and chairs exist. He is not one more 'thing' in the universe.)

What, then, can we say about contemporary humanism?

Humanists have a set of principles based on an idea of human significance, human value and human flourishing. The impression they give, especially to young minds, is that the humanist understanding of what it is to be human and what makes for human flourishing is somehow a scientific account, based on empirical observation, in contrast to a religious account, derived from revelation and requiring faith. In fact, contemporary humanism is a mix of science, value judgements and a good deal of faith – not unlike religion. Or, as John Gray has written with less charity, humanism is 'a pastiche of current scientific orthodoxy and pious hopes'.[9] The best way of dealing with it is, therefore, to expose this by submitting humanism to the same kind of critical scrutiny to which Christianity has so long been exposed.

An obvious starting point for considering humanist claims is to look at what they say about themselves. In 2009, the British Humanist Association produced some introductory literature for enquirers.[10] From this we can construct an outline of humanist philosophy. The key points are these:

- Humanism is a philosophy or way of life that puts human beings at the centre.
- The only authority human beings can appeal to is human reason.
- Beliefs should be proportionate to the evidence and an open mind should be kept if the evidence is inconclusive.
- There are universal values shared across human societies that arise out of human needs and the needs of society.
- All human beings have the capacity to think for themselves about morality.

- We should act in the interest of social harmony and the common good.
- Where there are conflicting values we should decide between them on the basis of the likely consequences.
- This world is all there is.
- The idea of life after death is incoherent.
- Our only survival is in the memories of others and in what we each achieve and leave behind.
- Life has no 'ultimate' or 'transcendent' meaning but only the meanings we each give to it.

This creed is now very influential and should be regarded as Christianity's principal, most attractive and most formidable rival in contemporary Britain. It occupies a place not unlike that occupied by Christianity in relation to Pharisaic Judaism in the first days of the Church.[11] The conflict between the emerging Church and the Pharisees was sharp precisely because they were in many respects ideologically/theologically so close. Similarly, I would argue, humanism is a creed very close to, and in some quite crucial respects even dependent on, the Christian understanding of human nature, the Christian idea of purpose in history and the Christian ethic. Terry Eagleton, Distinguished Professor of English Literature at Lancaster University, has indeed called it 'a continuation of God by other means'.[12]

The first thing to be noticed is that in its agnostic form – leaving open the question of God's existence – humanism makes it easier for people who have been influenced by religion at some point in their lives, such as their childhood, to make a more gradual transition from Christianity to unbelief. The break with a religious past, whether individual or collective, is less dramatic. The question of God is not finally closed, and the strong social and ethical flavour – in many ways mirroring contemporary Christianity's own humanist ethic – has great appeal. The temptation for many, therefore, is to see humanism as Christianity without supernaturalism and, crucially, without church. Then, after a while, the point of churchgoing is lost, and the transition from belief to unbelief may be the final, logical step. This makes it essential to unmask the many assumptions and value judgements that humanism makes that do not derive from any scientific account of the world and the human species but may well represent a Christian residue.

Humanism is an optimistic creed – some might say naively so. It is optimistic about the capacity of human reason to solve problems and move human society forward in ways that bring about greater flourishing – social harmony and the common good. There are other non-religious, atheistic accounts of human nature and human capacity that see both in far darker terms. Freud believed that the forces that control us are largely beyond our knowledge or ability to influence, lying deep within each individual. Marx believed that individual human lives were flotsam, tossed this way and that by strong currents of economic change that people were powerless to control.[13] By opting for a less pessimistic understanding of human beings and human capacity, humanism is taking a leap of faith rather than making its beliefs proportionate to the evidence.

As to post-Darwinian science, it only allows us to say that the human species, part of the animal kingdom, sharing a great deal of its DNA with the higher primates, but also lesser amounts with other forms of life, has emerged and so far survived because it has been able to adapt successfully to its changing environment. But that is no guarantee that the species will continue to survive whatever the future might bring – such as a period of prolonged global warming. James Lovelock, the environmental scientist and originator of the Gaia Theory, for example, believes that the evolutionary success of the human race – not recent industrialization alone – has inflicted such damage on the natural world that some form of global catastrophe for human communities is inevitable as the earth adjusts and human beings find they are powerless to reverse this.[14] Some Darwinian scientists would argue that human beings can no more direct their fate than any other species. Nor does science enable us to make any moral judgement about the value, significance or worth of this form of life, or allow us to speak about any particular human destiny. In so far as humanism gives value and significance to human life, its critics would see that as an unconscious reference to the Christian idea of humanity as made in God's image, and humanist optimism as a secular form of the Christian idea of providence.[15]

From a Christian perspective, what is so striking about contemporary secular humanism is that there is no reference to human sin, as there would be in any Christian account of human beings. On the face of it, this is a surprising and seriously flawed assessment, not least after a century – the twentieth century – that saw some of the bloodiest years in European if not world history, from two world wars to Pol Pot. Christianity does not have an optimistic view of human beings, but it does have a high view of them as made in God's image; and it does speak about the possibility of redemption. But for the generations born well after the Second World War, that have only known a time of relative peace and considerable plenty, talk of sin cuts across their sunny and optimistic view of human nature and the human future. Whether the 2008 banking crisis and economic recession will affect this attitude is hard to say, though at the time of writing, the banks have largely been saved and most people have avoided the worst effects of a contracting economy.

It also seems wildly optimistic for humanists to suppose that when human beings conflict over 'values' the matter can be settled by a consideration of 'consequences'. Those who disagree over conflicting values are just as likely to disagree over the consequences of holding and pursuing some values and not others. Consequences may be difficult to predict, but even if we could agree on what the consequences of any actions might be, we may still disagree on their relative desirability.

If humanism, then, embraces a utilitarian ethic, we can see how unconsciously dependent it often is on a type of Christian humanism, for there are other forms of utilitarianism that are very different from what the British Humanist Association stands for. The utilitarian philosopher Peter Singer, for example, argues strongly that once Christianity has been abandoned, two consequences follow: the privileging of the human species above other animals has to stop; and the idea that all human life is equally valuable and to be preserved at whatever cost is not justified.[16] There is nothing in a non-religious ethic, Singer believes, to justify using animals, especially the higher primates, for purposes of medical research (for the exclusive benefit of the human species). The Christian faith teaches that humans and not animals are made in God's image, and animals, while they are not to be treated cruelly, are for human use (St Thomas Aquinas). Without some such understanding, Singer argues, we are forced to conclude that animal experimentation is a form of speciesism on our part: we do it because we can, because we are more powerful than animals and can make use of them. It also follows that we should not eat them. Singer is an ethical vegetarian.

Singer argues that the religious assessment of human life as intrinsically valuable – made in God's image and loved by him – must also be left behind when Christianity is abandoned. Human life is not intrinsically valuable but has value only if it is life of a certain quality: it is rational, relational, self-conscious and so on. When these qualities are not present, as with a person in a persistent vegetative state or suffering from extreme dementia, there is no utilitarian argument for prolonging that life: it is not a life of any human quality or worth. We should have no ethical anxieties, therefore, about bringing such a life to an end through involuntary euthanasia. Far more contentiously, Singer has also argued for infanticide where a child suffers from some irreparable and devastating brain damage such that it cannot relate to others, has no self-awareness and can never have independent life. Again, involuntary euthanasia should be permitted and it is only a Christian memory of the sacredness of human life per se that, irrationally, prevents a truly secular society taking the obvious steps.

These references to a Christian legacy remind us of something important, namely that the Christian memory grows dimmer as the decades pass and the means of refreshing it cease to be available. One place where the seriousness of what we have done will begin to show itself is at the non-religious funeral service. If the worth of human life is to be measured by a utilitarian test in terms of what a person has done in and with his or her life (the relationships he or she has built, the contribution he or she has made to the community and so on), what are we to say about those who fail significantly? An extreme case may help to show what I mean. Some years ago, I officiated at the funeral of a young man who had killed himself and caused the death of others when he crashed the car he had stolen into an oncoming vehicle. It soon became clear when talking to the young man's mother that there was almost nothing positive in his life that we could talk about in any tribute. He had scarcely attended school. He had never had a job. He had no real friends, only people with whom he did drugs, got drunk and committed crimes. He had an uncontrollable temper and his mother was afraid of him. He had no hobbies or interests. And now he had killed other human beings through his drunken actions. It is hard to know how a society that relied on utilitarian assessments of worth could say anything that would bring any kind of comfort to this young man's mother and sister, or could supply any sort of meaning to anyone else caught up in his life. This is an extreme case, but many lives will be lived that will be found severely wanting if a utilitarian assessment is the only measure of worth, and the only meaning we can give to human life is the meaning we each forge for ourselves. The Christian funeral liturgy does not ground the worth of individuals on anything they have achieved or the kind of person they are, or on any human judgement about worth, but on the religious fact that they are made in God's image and God will redeem them even as he will judge them. There is a lot at stake when a society loses its religious traditions.

The Church in the twenty-first century, therefore, is facing a vigorous and alluring alternative faith in the form of secular humanism. There is also the strong possibility that agnostic humanism acts as a conveyor belt between Christianity and atheism. It needs confronting. With each generation that passes, more and more people become distanced from Christian prayer and worship and the Christian capital is depleted further; indifference is not arrested but becomes a way of life. But it is not only the rising generations that are influenced by secular humanism, though they may have fewer Christian resources to draw on. I have noticed in recent years a growing number of older people who have confided during the course of some or other piece of research or when visiting to arrange the funeral of a relative that their Christian convictions had weakened. If this is an accurate reflection of what may be happening, it runs counter to what has previously been thought, that people became more religious with age. They had shared this with no one, not even their spouse and certainly not their minister. Needless to say, the concerns they had were never addressed in sermons or house groups. Intellectually, as far as faith was concerned they had ploughed a lonely furrow. Yet their neighbour in the pew was doing the same. This is a serious issue.

The resilience of the chaplaincy role

It is still possible for older generations to be indifferent towards organized religion in the belief that they can fall back on the half-remembered religious meanings and religious responses they already possess as a result of some earlier acquaintance with Christianity. They have not resorted to alternative spiritualities and still call upon the ministry of the Church at particular moments. They regard themselves as Christians and see the ordained ministry as a kind of national chaplaincy service or clerical arm of the welfare state (and are thus thoroughgoing erastians). We see this when people have to deal with critical moments of transition in their lives and ask for the occasional offices – baptisms at the birth of a child, weddings, funerals. We see it when they are prepared to accept the ministry of the Church at times of national or local celebration or crisis – a coronation, a Remembrance Day service, prayers for the victims of some tragedy. Transcendent meanings can lie buried and unobserved in people until the need to draw on them arises. Then the Church's ministry is explicitly called for and appreciated – as long as it is sensitively and appropriately offered. I have written at greater length elsewhere about the continuing significance of the pastoral offices.[17] One comment on an ordinary funeral in a small, rural, English parish church by an avowed atheist illustrates how day-to-day ministry is still appreciated, when it is done well. Matthew Parris wrote this about the funeral of someone who had once been kind to him:

> In an astonishing break with Anglican tradition, the Vicar read the epistle (St Paul's 'We do not live to ourselves alone, and we do not die to ourselves alone') with meaning, feeling and timing; and delivered an address that showed a real effort to find out about and understand the deceased. Heads nodded among us mourners outside, all moved, close family and friends in floods of tears; and we sang 'All Things Bright and Beautiful', knowing how Ken loved trees.[18]

(I am not sure whether Parris's swipe at the clergy's general ability to read meaningfully is wholly justified; but we ought to take note.) Two relatively recent illustrations of other occasional services will suffice to make the same general point.

In August 1997, Diana, Princess of Wales was killed in a car crash in Paris, having been pursued by paparazzi. There was an enormous outpouring of grief across the nation. The funeral service was held in Westminster Abbey and was carefully constructed by the Dean and his staff to reflect something of the personality of the Princess and to give expression to the emotions generated in so many by her early and tragic death. One striking instance of that was the performance of an adapted version of the song, 'Candle in the wind' (written originally about Marilyn Monroe), by Sir Elton John. In addition, the Princess's sister read a favourite poem and her brother delivered a (contentious) eulogy. There were also more traditional hymns and anthems, Scripture readings and prayers. Many strong emotions were in play – from deep sorrow to considerable anger. It was generally accepted by most secular commentators that the Church of England had handled this difficult national occasion appropriately and well, enabling people to express in a controlled way those strong emotions.

Then in 2002, a school caretaker, Ian Huntley, murdered two young girls, Holly Wells and Jessica Chapman, in the English market town of Soham in Cambridgeshire. The nation was transfixed by the crime. A photograph of the two friends dressed in red football shirts appeared on every news bulletin and in every newspaper for many weeks. The parish church in Soham was soon being visited by hundreds of people moved by the story of the girls' disappearance and then murder. The vicar, the Revd Tim Alban Jones, made it possible for the visitors to leave flowers in the churchyard and light candles in the church. He knew the families and arranged sensitive funeral and memorial services. In this way, the grief of the families and local community, together with the sympathy and sorrow of countless numbers of strangers, was able to be expressed in ways that allowed everyone to find some consolation.

In the case of both Princess Diana and the Soham deaths, the Church of England and its clergy had acted in accordance with those principles that were embedded in the Book of Common Prayer. The services enabled a range of people, believers and unbelievers alike, to express grief in their own way; yet they also held before people the possibility of transcendent meaning.

However, these opportunities for ministry by the Church require two conditions to be met. First, the Church, particularly the Church of England, has to be willing to be as inclusive as possible on these occasions, and its clergy and congregations have to have a genuine interest in and commitment to their parishes – the chaplaincy role. Ministry is offered to those who are not part of the regular Sunday congregation. We should note in this regard that the British people have long memories. Some inner-city areas had for many decades a folk memory of the way some Anglo-Catholic clergy wore themselves out in the slums of Victorian and Edwardian Britain and the terraced streets that accompanied successive waves of industrial expansion. When they died, hundreds that had never been to church services but did appreciate the lives of unselfish devotion the clergy had shown turned out to witness their funeral processions. It was this life of service, rather than the doctrine or ritual of those churches, that endeared the clergy to their working-class parishioners and made ministry possible. This was all the more remarkable when we recall that many of these clergy came from a quite different social background from those among whom they ministered. Others remember a devoted civic ministry in churches such as St Martin in the Fields, or the work of wartime chaplains. In country parishes too, the faithful parson, showing a friendly and sympathetic face to all, built up reservoirs of affection and trust that are vital if occasional ministry is to be sought and offered. In each case, the influence of the clergy extended well beyond their own time, building attitudes towards the Church and its ordained ministers that passed from one generation to another.

In the second place, ministry has to take into account the actual needs that the pastoral offices and occasional services are meeting. The Church has its own purposes and intentions in baptisms, weddings and funerals; but those who continue to seek out the pastoral offices have theirs, and clergy need to be sensitive to them. So, for example, a single mother bringing her child for baptism is committing herself to raise the child in the Christian faith – as the liturgy declares – but she will also have other urgent needs that this rite will satisfy. Perhaps she needs to give her child the same start in life that she believes a child with two supportive parents will have; perhaps she just needs affirming in her own ability as mother; perhaps she needs affirming before family and friends and wider community. Clergy who have the patience to build trust with those who come for pastoral services, and are sensitive to their particular needs, can shape prayers or emphasize aspects of the liturgy accordingly.

There is one further aspect of this particular ministry that should be noted. It can only be successful in the parish if clergy are prepared to commit themselves to an area for a relatively long period of time. But it is not easy for clergy to sustain a long ministry without finding fresh projects. In theory, ministerial reviews should function as a means of auditing and stimulating, though whether those who conduct them see them in this light is another matter.

This continuing acceptance of the chaplaincy role is also appreciated in those contexts where the term 'chaplain' is explicitly used, particularly in the armed forces, in hospices and hospitals. In 2009, the National Secular Society ran a vigorous campaign to stop the NHS funding hospital chaplaincies, on the grounds that a state enterprise had no business supporting religious functionaries and that the money (which they estimated at £26 million per annum) could be better spent employing 1,300 additional nurses or 2,645 extra cleaners. The president of the society, Terry Sanderson, said that if people wanted a chaplain they could send for the local vicar, priest, rabbi or imam. On the whole, the public was not convinced and many, including many non-believers, commented on the help chaplains had been to them. The secularists misunderstood the role of the chaplain, which was well summarized by Melanie Reid writing in *The Times*:

> Chaplains, in my experience, do not proselytize; they simply afford patients the kind of time, care and compassion that medical staff can no longer give them ... it is non-religious people, lost in a crisis, who need chaplains the most ... it is the injured, the dying and the bereaved, who seek not necessarily God, but a little kindness and succour at their time of greatest need.[19]

In other words, there are circumstances in which a public Church is acceptable in a democracy, even among many non-believers. But it does require clergy to be sensitive to what those unspoken terms and conditions are: they can offer a pastoral ministry, justified in religious terms, as long as they do not discriminate against those who do not share their religion and do not seek to convert. This leads us directly to the question of the establishment of the Church of England in a more diverse society.

Establishment in a diverse society

The role that religion should play in public life has become a contentious issue in recent years on both sides of the Atlantic, not least because Western societies are becoming increasingly diverse. If the nineteenth century was the age of the pluralism of the elite, the twentieth century saw the advance of democratic pluralism.[20] The issue, however, arises for different reasons in different countries, as a comparison of the United States and Britain shows.

The constitutional position of religion in the two countries is very different, but also highly misleading. The United States has a religious culture but no established religion; Britain is a secular society but has an established Church. The first amendment to the US constitution makes it clear that there is to be a separation of Church and state:

Congress shall make no law respecting an establishment of religion, or prohibiting the free exercise thereof; or abridging the freedom of speech, or of the press; or the right of the people peaceably to assemble, and to petition the government for a redress of grievances.[21]

Given the position of the constitution – the state supports no religion – it may seem strange to a British audience that an American President could express himself in the terms that George W. Bush used at the conclusion of his State of the Union address in 2003:

Americans are a free people, who know that freedom is the right of every person and the future of every nation. The liberty we prize is not America's gift to the world; it is God's gift to humanity. We Americans have faith in ourselves, but not in ourselves alone. We do not claim to know all the ways of Providence, yet we can trust in them, placing our confidence in the loving God behind all of life and all of history. May he guide us now, and may God continue to bless the United States of America.[22]

This is an unambiguous declaration of religious faith, and looks to divine guidance in the conduct of public affairs. But was this merely a religious rhetorical flourish, designed to please those conservative Christians who had turned out in considerable numbers to vote for the President in the election of 2000, not really signifying that the Bible could act as a kind of manifesto? In fact, when we turn to Bush's speeches that were directly concerned with political–ethical issues, the appeal to the biblical tradition was just as direct. For instance, in a talk to the American people in 2001, the President justified his opposition to stem-cell research in these words:

I also believe human life is a sacred gift from our Creator. I worry about a culture that devalues life and believe as your President I have an important obligation to foster and encourage respect for life in America and throughout the world.[23]

While this President may have been more inclined than others to use overtly religious language, the appeal to religion is not at all unusual in presidential speeches, nor is it typical of Republicans rather than Democrats.[24] Bill Clinton, for example, concluded his 1999 State of the Union address with similar religious sentiments and motifs:

My fellow Americans, this is our moment. Let us lift up our eyes as one nation, and from the mountain-top of this American century, look ahead to the next one, asking God's blessing on our endeavors and on our beloved country.[25]

His words echo those of the psalmist: 'I will lift up mine eyes unto the hills, from whence cometh my help.'[26] The reference to the mountain top is also a biblical reference that would only make complete sense to people who knew the Old Testament account of the death of Moses.[27] Even Barack Obama, who will probably not seek to justify policy decisions by quoting directly from the Christian tradition in the manner of George W. Bush, his predecessor, nevertheless stated in his inauguration speech: 'This is the source of our confidence – the knowledge that God calls on us to shape an uncertain destiny.' He ended by asserting that God's grace was upon the American people and invoking God's blessing.

The misunderstanding of the United States by the British results in part from seeing its constitutional separation of Church and state from the perspective of the European experience. Modern, democratic nations came about in much of Europe only after bitter struggles between Church and state. This was especially true of France, where the (Roman Catholic) Church made a serious error at the time of the revolution in 1789 by allying itself with the forces of privilege and reaction – monarchy and aristocracy. This created a profound and widespread anti-clericalism as well as republicanism. Denis Diderot summed this up when he opined that people would never be free until the last king was strangled with the entrails of the last priest. Church and state were separated as part of wider attempts to diminish, if not destroy altogether, the influence of religion. The policy of ensuring that all state institutions are secular – known as *laïcité* – is still rigorously enforced in France.[28] But the separation of Church and state in the United States was pursued for the opposite reason: not to emasculate religion, but to enable the many different varieties of Christianity to co-exist, and have equal chances to build churches and membership, by denying a privileged position to any one of them. To the casual European observer, this formal constitutional arrangement might suggest the desire for a secular culture. In fact, the whole point of the constitution was to produce the conditions in which every church could compete for members; it made each denomination and congregation entrepreneurial, lively and evangelistic, for otherwise they would not survive. And it led to religion flourishing, though without the possibility of any church exercising the monopolistic and oppressive power enjoyed by an established Church. That this happened would have gladdened, not dismayed, the hearts of the founders. Whatever the constitution says, we would have to conclude that the United States is a religious culture in which the Christian faith can make a contribution to public debate unapologetically and directly. This is not so in Britain.

Most of the biblical references that are often the stock-in-trade of American politicians would be entirely lost on contemporary British listeners. With few people attending churches, the Bible is no longer heard, and it is no longer read in either the home or the school, despite religious education being a compulsory subject – something that can mislead Americans about the place of religion in the lives of the British. Similarly, the invocation of the divine blessing by a politician in office would either startle a British audience or be treated as little more than a rather old-fashioned, meaningless and embarrassing piety, left over from a previously religious age. The idea that when a US President asks God's blessing it is meant in all sincerity, is something most British people would find almost impossible to comprehend.

What this brief sketch of American and British politics and constitution makes clear is that whether or not a political culture is or is not religious has little to do with what the constitution says. The United States has a religious political culture in a way that is quite inconceivable in Britain. Nevertheless, the Church of England and the Church of Scotland remain established. Can this be justified any longer, given the highly plural nature of modern Britain?

We should notice, first, that 'establishment' has no fixed meaning. In Scotland, the Church of Scotland is the national Church in the sense that it receives official recognition by government, it has a chaplaincy role towards all the Scottish people, which it discharges through a parish system, and the monarch sometimes attends meetings of the Kirk. But the monarch is not the Supreme Governor and the government does not seek to influence Church appointments or scrutinize Church business. In England, the Church of England was created by Act of Parliament and some of its legislation – mainly that of a financial nature – has to receive the consent of the Houses of Parliament.[29] The monarch is a member of the Church of England and also its Supreme Governor. Bishops are chosen by the crown on the recommendation of the Prime Minister, who in turn consults the Church (though Gordon Brown as Prime Minister refused to exercise this right). Since 'establishment' is not a fixed idea, it is capable of further development, should that be thought necessary.

In the past, establishment gave the Church of England considerable privileges. Few of those remain, though some do, and these give the Church a certain access to those in positions of power and influence at every level of society. The Church understood that together with these privileges went certain responsibilities. These responsibilities have been refined over time and include: acting as chaplain to all and not just those who attend services (as discussed above); acting in an ecumenical spirit on civic and national occasions; representing the interests of all Christians in the corridors of power; speaking, sparingly, to the powerful in the name of the weak and oppressed.[30] This was how the Church of England believed it could fulfil the mission of the Church in England. This was its particular vocation, though since it receives no state support in the way that some continental churches do through the church tax, the role has become harder to fulfil. A new chapter has now opened up with the appearance of large numbers of adherents of other faiths. If the Church wishes to maintain its established role, it will have to make further adjustments, stretching the idea of ecumenism to embrace those minority faiths as well. For the moment, there is every sign that the other faiths welcome this – it means that the state recognizes a public role for religion – and there is no great pressure from them for the national Church to be disestablished. Pressure does come, however, from secular humanists, atheists and the cultured despisers. This will grow as the years go by, and much will depend on how successful it will be in converting a religiously indifferent public into a hostile one. The process can be accelerated by the Church of England itself if it gives up on its chaplaincy role or believes there are advantages to be had for the Church's mission by walking away from this historic role, or thinks that its ability to be prophetic is best served by breaking all links with the state. The Archbishop of Canterbury has already given signals that he would not fight vigorously to frustrate disestablishment, so we must assume that the signs are not encouraging if one still sees value for both Church and nation in the present arrangements.

The principal objection of the secularist to establishment – in fact to any public role for religion – is that the state must remain neutral in the matter of belief. It can privilege neither believers nor unbelievers, but must hold the ring for both. From this a number of things follow: it becomes impossible for the state school to teach any particular belief system or religious faith as true, or to support acts of religious worship; no church can be established; religion has to be treated as a private and in no sense a public commitment. At first glance this seems a powerful argument, but is there more to be said?

At present what we have in England is a 'lite' form of establishment, the result of a gradual erosion and surrender of privileges over several centuries. At one time objections to Anglican establishment would have come from other Christians because of the form it then took. The Act of Uniformity in 1662 attempted to impose the Book of Common Prayer on the whole country. Those who would not conform, who went on to found what became Presbyterian, Congregationalist and Baptist churches, are still sometimes referred to as 'Nonconformists'. For almost 200 years, Nonconformists were seriously disadvantaged: they could not be educated at either Oxford or Cambridge; they had to be married according to the rites and ceremonies of the Church of England; they could not become Members of Parliament or civil servants and so on.

Roman Catholics and Jews were similarly disadvantaged. Most of this has now gone.

But can even 'establishment lite' be justified in a modern democratic state? The answer probably turns on the extent to which we think the British identity, including its modern democratic identity, is the result in part of Christianity; and on whether that identity would begin to be seriously eroded and changed in ways that the British people do not want if religion were to have no public role. I would want to argue that the form democracy has taken in the UK has in very large measure resulted from its Christian and specifically Protestant inheritance. Christianity has meant that the British people have acknowledged that all people – including kings and prime ministers – are ultimately accountable to one who stands above and beyond all politics. Protestantism asserts that all human institutions, including sacred ones, have erred and are never infallible. Since the end of the Civil War, the British have had to work out how a people can live together despite strongly held religious and political differences. British Protestantism has learnt to breathe an ecumenical spirit – an ecumenical spirit that has now extended to embrace all the world's faiths. This is the religious framework within which British democracy has developed and continues to develop. It has served the country well, not least in recent years as the nation has had to come to terms with all the challenges that a multi-cultural and multi-faith society brings.

Today, however, establishment presents the old Nonconformists and other denominations with something of a dilemma. If they feel it important to have religion acknowledged in public life and not simply regarded as a private matter as the secularists demand, it has to take some institutional form. In England, the form this has taken is the establishment of the Church of England. This is the price other Christians pay for keeping a religious presence in public life, and they are prepared to pay it as long as the national Church maintains a chaplaincy approach, protects their interests and seeks their inclusion whenever possible. As long as the other denominations and now other religions are content with this arrangement, and as long as a critical mass of the British people are able to associate themselves with Christianity, establishment can still make sense and can still be justified. The choice is not 'the secular state' or 'establishment'; there is a very British, middle way: establishment lite.

Opposition to establishment comes also, however, from within the Church of England itself – and there is similar opposition among Presbyterians to the Church of Scotland's position.[31] The arguments in England are the same as those mounted in the nineteenth century by the Tractarians. They objected to the loss of freedom implied by the state's attempt to suppress Irish bishoprics. The Church does lose some of its freedom by having to submit legislation to Parliament. However, the theoretical possibility that it would be more able to speak prophetically if it were not established has to be balanced with a clear-eyed view of just how marginal a disestablished Church of England would quickly become. The bishops may think they command media attention because of the sagacity and brilliance of what they have to say; the truth is that, with few exceptions, any impact they have arises from the fact that they are bishops of the established Church with seats in the House of Lords, whose Supreme Governor is the monarch. A serious rebranding of the Church would have to follow disestablishment; it is one thing for the established Church to call itself the Church of England, but quite another for one Christian sect among many to make such a bold if not arrogant claim.

The priorities for ordained ministry

In this final section I will draw together the threads of a number of arguments and set out what I believe tomorrow's ordained ministry will need to look like if it is to meet the challenges posed by twenty-first century Britain. If the Church is to resource the British people spiritually and retain any hold on their affections in the coming years, it must make the two aspects of ministry I discuss below its priorities. I have concentrated on two priorities rather than a set of recommendations: having spent a large part of my life both giving and receiving recommendations on various committees and boards, I know how easy it is to lose focus when presented with long lists of things to do. We need to be clear about where the major priorities lie. If we can grasp that, the details will begin to suggest themselves. But if we lose that focus we shall dissipate our energies.

A teaching ministry: the intellectual contribution of the clergy

First, in a time of no religion the Church must keep alive the memory of Jesus Christ. Does this sound too trite or too obvious? If we feel it does, we need to recall what it means to say that we live in a time of no religion – the theme of Chapter 1 above. A time of no religion is a time when for a majority of people religion no longer plays a lively or significant role in shaping how they think about themselves and the world, and in consequence it is neglected and forgotten. Those who have lived through the 60 or so years that began with the end of the Second World War have experienced a time when the nation began to walk away from the Church – people stopped being interested in organized religion – and to lose its collective memory of the Christian faith.

156

This led one writer to speak of the 'death' of Christian Britain, by which he meant the marginalization of Christianity in the culture generally. It was not just that people stopped going to church in any numbers but that Christian assumptions and Christian values were ceasing to have influence over all aspects of life.

The importance of memory for keeping traditions and ideas alive is a frequent theme in the writings of the Czech novelist, Milan Kundera. He notes how on taking power in eastern Europe after the Second World War, the Communists set about rewriting history by systematically erasing the collective memory of the pre-Communist past – what Kundera calls 'organized forgetting'.[32] The authorities did not want people to have any reminders of alternative ways of organizing political life. Anything that awkwardly spoke of alternatives had to be eliminated. Church buildings were one obvious target, but so were public monuments and statues. They had to be replaced. In the end, the Communists were even re-fashioning their own period of history. A striking example is the story of the historic photograph of the founding of the Czech Communist state in February 1948. The original showed Klement Gottwald, the party leader, standing on the balcony of the Baroque palace in Prague flanked by his comrades, making the announcement. It was a cold day and one colleague, Comrade Clementis, placed his fur cap on Gottwald's uncovered head. But within a few years Clementis had fallen from grace and was arrested. When the photograph was subsequently reissued, Clementis was airbrushed out. He was made to disappear, as if he had never been; only his cap remained on Gottwald's head.

We are seeing Christianity airbrushed out of our own history with only an occasional residual reminder, like Clementis's cap. Is that too much of an exaggeration? The signs are there for us all to see, and have been for some time. I was at a social occasion shortly after the turn of the century, talking to a lecturer in history at one of the newer universities. She spoke about the difficulties she had experienced teaching the English Civil War to contemporary students who knew nothing about the Christian faith. A colleague in the English department experienced the same problem teaching Shakespeare. So they had approached the Religious Studies department for help with a basic course on the Bible and Christian Doctrine. 'Did it go well?' I asked. 'It never happened. They are not subjects the department teaches and they didn't feel confident enough to do anything,' was the depressing reply. Behind this sad state of affairs lie the years of neglect: the collapse of the Sunday Schools, the disappearance of Christian acts of worship in schools and biblical knowledge from Religious Education syllabuses, the secularization of church colleges of higher education, the failure to encourage serious study of Christianity in many parishes.

We make sense of our lives by weaving together particular memories to make a narrative or story. But memories are not acquired once and for all. They have to be constantly rehearsed, renewed and refreshed. You can see this process at work within families. The reason we value photographs as much as we do is because of the part they play in refreshing memory and helping us to tell the family story. Each family is a community of memory. This is why families will spend time at Christmas or wedding anniversaries or birthdays getting the family photograph album out and reminiscing. In this way the family's story about itself is told and retold and added to.

The analogy of the family constructing its story points us to the fact that this sort of remembering is never simply a matter of calling to mind. Discrete memories are selected and made to fit into the larger story. The past is recalled and understood in a particular way. That way of understanding may subtly change or, sometimes, less subtly, be changed, as the story is reiterated. In this way the sense of who this family is, of identity and meaning, is built up. In a similar way the Christian story was once told and retold. As far as most people are concerned, it is no longer being heard, and therefore it is only a matter of time before the memory has gone completely. The death of Christian Britain will then be a reality.

This national self-induced amnesia has been aided and abetted by the Church, for apart from the evangelicals, insufficient thought has been given by clergy to providing opportunities for lay Christians to learn more about their faith and its application to life. Yet historically, both evangelicals and Anglo-Catholics understood the need for systematic and careful teaching. So the first priority has to lie there – and those parts of the Church that are inexperienced in good educational methods will need to learn from the evangelicals who have produced excellent teaching materials and thoughtful teachers. But a large part of that teaching means helping contemporary Christians respond to the intellectual challenges of the times. Above all, this involves taking seriously the threat to Christianity that secular humanism now poses – something that the evangelicals have tended to underestimate along with everyone else. Secular humanism must be recognized as more than a denial of Christianity, as I have sought to show: it is a vibrant, alternative faith. It is making considerable progress, among thoughtful people in every generation.

A pastoral ministry: understanding the role of chaplain to the nation

Second, I have suggested above that the traditional representative of the Church of England – the parson – remains the most effective way for the Church to fulfil its pastoral vocation in the immediate future. This requires an ordained ministry equipped with particular skills. Here I would like to highlight what seems to me the key skill-set needed for this pastoral ministry.

Timothy Jenkins, Dean and Fellow of Jesus College, Cambridge, has noted how the skills needed for pastoral ministry are not unlike those required in some other professions. The crossovers with social work and counselling are obvious, but Jenkins, writing about his time as a curate, has found interesting parallels with other disciplines, in particular his own training as a social anthropologist. The anthropologist needs first to be able to describe accurately what he or she sees and hears – a tough intellectual challenge. He must pay close attention, watching, listening, seeking to understand. This requires great patience and the cultivation of a mind that is interested and curious about fellow human beings. In many respects, it is also the mind of a novelist who must do more than observe but must seek to get inside the skin of other people, experiencing the world as they experience it, seeing as they see.

It also necessitates a willingness not to push one's own point of view. As religious professionals this means not introducing overtly religious themes too quickly; being engaged yet, in a sense, detached. Timothy Jenkins calls this 'not bringing God into a situation'. There is a tendency for people to give clergy the answers they think they want to hear. If religious professionals are too quick in 'bringing God into a situation' then that will dictate the way a conversation goes – and important matters will be pushed to one side. Above all, the ordained minister needs to notice when he (or she) is getting things right and when he is not understanding.[33]

All of this requires that the clergy live locally. It is only by being part of a community over a period of time that the minister is able to put into words the truth about the life of particular individuals and communities – as the classical model of the parson suggests. He does not have to know every individual personally; but he does have to know first-hand what it is to live in this place rather than another. It is because the minister is embedded in this way that he has the authority to speak about individual lives on an occasion such as a funeral, or to speak on behalf of an entire community at particular moments of celebration or tragedy. Jenkins calls this knowledge 'embodied, contextual and personal'.

We should not underestimate the difficulties some clergy will have with this. Clergy often feel they are failing in their vocation if they are not immediately and directly raising the question of religion in whatever day-to-day situations they find themselves. The pressure to do this has increased in recent decades as the need for evangelism has been stressed. However, if clergy can learn patient attentiveness, noting when they have understood correctly and when not, they will acquire the skills that enable them to have a much more valuable pastoral ministry in contemporary Britain; and then when people feel able and ready to ask for spiritual counsel, they will ask.

The consequences for initial training

Recommendations for clergy training generally take the form of adding to what is already in timetables and syllabuses. This is increasingly unrealistic in a time of diminishing resources. I want to suggest a radical pruning and refocusing, though I can do no more than hint at new directions. The two areas outlined above – intellectual challenge and pastoral ministry – should be the principal focus.

The intellectual training of clergy is critical if the battle for minds as well as hearts is to be won. Clearly clergy need some grounding in what were once called biblical studies, doctrine, liturgy and Church history, but the emphasis needs to shift towards the issues that face Christianity in today's society. So, for example, no student should leave initial training without having explored the role the Bible and doctrine play in the life of the contemporary Christian. They should be thoroughly conversant with the kind of arguments that the humanist uses against the idea of sacred Scripture and the Christian understanding of God and human beings. They should be skilled in deploying biblical and doctrinal resources to respond to the ethical issues that confront us.

Most ordinands today are very different from the inexperienced young men (there were no women) that entered theological colleges 40 years ago. It was right that they should be given a chance to broaden their knowledge and experience in practical ways through a variety of placements. (It must be said that very few placements in the past have been in the places where the majority of worshippers spend their working lives – as local government officers, bank clerks, journalists, lorry drivers and so on.) This is now unnecessary, and much financial resource could be saved by stopping it. Of far more value is helping these generally older men and women reflect on experiences they already have in the light of the Christian faith – not least because these are the skills they will need in the parish. It is a frequent complaint of ordinands that their tutors do not know how to utilize the student's knowledge and experience even if they know about it. Liturgy too needs to be seen not as an exercise in archaeology but in making God findable in a Church that has a national chaplaincy role. The focus should be helping students see why their own predilections in worship may have to be sacrificed or modified for the sake of those they serve, both inside and outside the regular congregation.

And finally . . .

We have ended where we began, with the question, 'What are clergy for?' I have argued that clergy serve the mission and ministry of the Church, which is to make God possible. The form that takes in each new era will change as the Church seeks to respond to changes in society and culture. Part of that change involves the clergy refocusing their ministry. In the first part of this book I sought to show what some of the cultural shifts have been and the challenges they present to Christianity in the twenty-first century. In the second part we explored some of the models of ministry that have been found in the Church in the past and that continue to exercise an influence. I suggested what seems to me to be of lasting importance and value in each that could contribute towards the renewal of ordained ministry for these times. Although I began by noting clerical anxieties, I end by saying clergy should not be discouraged: people continue to seek the ministry of the Church even in these more secular times. But if we are to offer them bread and not a stone, the ordained minister must understand the seriousness of the intellectual challenge from secular humanism on the one hand and, on the other, what it means to offer ministry to all, in the way that Jesus offered ministry to all.

Can the clergy do it? The jury is out.

Notes

Introduction

1 There are exceptions, such as: Martyn Percy, *Clergy: The Origin of Species* (London: Continuum, 2006).

2 Of course, neither the Society of Friends (Quakers) nor the Salvation Army has an ordained ministry.

3 Frank Field, 'God and the cop-out culture: a review of Alan Billings, *Secular Lives, Sacred Hearts*', *The Tablet*, 22 October 2005.

4 Martyn Percy speaks of a sense of 'bewilderment' in Percy, *Clergy*, p. 7. See R. Towler and A. Coxon, *The Fate of the Anglican Clergy* (London: Macmillan, 1979).

5 Hugh Dickinson, 'What our bishops lack', *Church Times*, 9 February 1996, p. 12. *New Directions*, Vol. 1 No. 9, February 1966, p. 4.

6 John Pritchard, *The Life and Work of a Priest* (London: SPCK, 2007), p. 25.

7 Figures from <www.cofe.anglican.org/info/statistics/>.

8 Camilla Cavendish, an award-winning columnist for *The Times*, has been very critical of the fact that decisions affecting children are taken by family courts in secret, preventing public scrutiny.

9 In December 2008, the Director of Children's Services in the London Borough of Haringey was dismissed by the council because her department, allegedly, had not recognized that a child was being abused, despite 60 visits, and had failed to take him into care. The child was subsequently found dead in his cot and his mother, her boyfriend and a lodger were convicted of causing or allowing his death. The 'Baby P' case attracted huge publicity over many weeks and was generally thought to have demoralized the social work profession, whom the public held responsible.

10 Frank Wright, *The Pastoral Nature of the Ministry* (London: SCM, 1980), p. 1.

11 Wesley Carr, *Brief Encounters* (London: SPCK, 1985) and *The Priestlike Task* (London: SPCK, 1989) are exceptions.

12 I am, of course, aware that not all religion is concerned with the sacred in this sense.

13 Frank Furedi, *Therapy Culture: Cultivating Vulnerability in an Anxious Age* (London: Routledge, 2004), p. 1.

14 Helen Oppenheimer, *Finding and Following: Talking with Children about God* (London: SCM, 1994). The phrase was first used in Helen Oppenheimer, 'Making God Findable', in Giles Ecclestone (ed.), *The Parish Church?* (London: The Grubb Institute/Mowbray, 1988).

1 Understanding the context

1 This is discussed in Charles Taylor, *A Secular Age* (Cambridge, MA and London: Belknap, 1997), p. 426; Martyn Percy, *Clergy: The Origin of Species* (London: Continuum, 2006), pp. 76ff.

2 Quoted in Geoffrey Best, *Mid-Victorian Britain 1851–75* (London: Fontana, 1985), p. 10.

3 Exodus 20.8.

4 The reference is to Grace Davie, *Religion in Britain since 1945: Believing without Belonging* (London: Blackwell, 1994).

5 Steve Bruce, *Religion in Modern Britain* (Oxford: OUP, 1995). For information on the denominations, see Davie, *Religion in Britain since 1945*, pp. 45–6.

6 Hugh McLeod, *Religion and the People of Western Europe 1789–1970* (Oxford: OUP, 1981), p. 134.

7 Michael P. Hornsby-Smith, *Roman Catholics in England* (Cambridge: CUP, 1987).

8 See P. Brierley and D. Longley (eds), *UK Christian Handbook, 1992–3* (MARC Europe).

9 Cited in Owen Chadwick, *The Victorian Church, Part Two: 1860–1901* (London: SCM, 1972), p. 224.

10 For the 1851 Census figures see Owen Chadwick, *The Victorian Church, Part One: 1829–59* (London: SCM, 1971), pp. 363–9.

11 Horace Mann, *Census of Great Britain, 1851. Religious Worship. England and Wales. Report and Tables*, British Parliamentary Papers, Population 10, 1852–3 (reprinted Shannon: Irish University Press, 1970).

12 Robin Gill, *Competing Convictions* (London: SCM, 1989); *The Myth of the Empty Church* (London: SPCK, 1993); *The Empty Church Re-visited: Explorations in Pastoral, Practical and Empirical Theology* (London: Ashgate, 2nd edn, 2003).

13 John Henry Newman, *Apologia Pro Vita Sua* (New York: Norton, 1968), p. 188. Owen Chadwick, *The Secularization of the European Mind in the Nineteenth Century* (Cambridge: CUP, 1975). R. L. Brett, *Faith and Doubt: Religion and Secularisation in Literature from Wordsworth to Larkin* (Macon, GA: Mercer University Press; Cambridge: James Clarke & Co., 1997). Anthony Symondson (ed.), *The Victorian Crisis of Faith* (London: SPCK, 1970). A. O. J. Cockshut, *The Unbelievers: English Agnostic Thought 1840–1890* (London: Collins, 1964).

14 Studdert Kennedy's poetry is a witness to this rethinking. He anticipated Jürgen Moltmann's *Crucified God* in his 'rough rhymes' (as he called them), where he emphasizes the suffering of God in Christ. This is the poem 'Comrade God' in *The Sorrows of God and Other Poems* (London: Hodder & Stoughton, 1921):

> Thou who dost dwell in depths of timeless being,
> Watching the years as moments passing by,
> Seeing the things that lie beyond our seeing,
> Constant, unchanged, as aeons dawn and die;
> Thou who canst count the stars upon their courses,
> Holding them all in the hollow of Thy hand,

Lord of the world with its myriad of forces
Seeing the hills as single grains of sand;
Art Thou so great that this our bitter crying
Sounds in Thine ears like sorrow of a child?
Hast Thou looked down on centuries of sighing,
And, like a heartless mother, only smiled?
Since in Thy sight to-day is as to-morrow,
And while we strive Thy victory is won,
Hast Thou no tears to shed upon our sorrow?
Art Thou a staring splendour like the sun?
Dost Thou not heed the helpless sparrow's falling?
Canst Thou not see the tears that women weep?
Canst Thou not hear Thy little children calling?
Dost Thou not watch above them as they sleep?
Then, O my God, Thou art too great to love me,
Since Thou dost reign beyond the reach of tears.
Calm and serene as the cruel stars above me,
High and remote from human hopes and fears.
Only in Him can I find home to hide me,
Who on the Cross was slain to rise again;
Only with Him, my Comrade God, beside me,
Can I go forth to war with sin and pain.

15 Quoted in P. Brierley and V. Hiscock (eds), *UK Christian Handbook 1994–5* (London: Christian Research Association, 1993), p. 251.
16 The theory is vigorously defended and reiterated in Steve Bruce, *God is Dead: Secularization in the West* (Oxford: Blackwell, 2002).
17 Roger Finke, 'An Unsecular America', in Steve Bruce (ed.), *Religion and Modernization* (Oxford: OUP, 1992), pp. 154–5. America is changing, however. The American Religious Identification survey indicates that the number of self-identified Christians has fallen from 86 to 76 per cent in ten years. Cited in Jon Meacham, *Newsweek*, 13 April 2009.
18 See David Martin, *Forbidden Revolutions: Pentecostalism in Latin America, Catholicism in Eastern Europe* (London: SPCK, 1996).
19 See Davie, *Religion in Britain since 1945*.
20 See Bruce, *Religion and Modernization*, chapter 3.
21 The spirituality of the New Age is documented in Paul Heelas, *The New Age Movement* (Oxford: Blackwell, 1996).
22 Paul Heelas and Linda Woodhead, *The Spiritual Revolution: Why Religion is Giving Way to Spirituality* (Oxford: Blackwell, 2004).
23 Steve Bruce describes secular attitudes in this way in Bruce, *God is Dead*. Bruce believes indifference is the characteristic mark of modern Britain towards religion.
24 The point is made in Alasdair MacIntyre and Paul Ricoeur, *The Religious Significance of Atheism* (New York: Columbia University Press, 1969).
25 When Jesus came to Golgotha they hanged Him on a tree,
They drave great nails through hands and feet, and made a Calvary;

They crowned Him with a crown of thorns, red were His wounds and
deep,
For those were crude and cruel days, and human flesh was cheap.

When Jesus came to Birmingham they simply passed Him by,
They never hurt a hair of Him, they only let Him die;
For men had grown more tender, and they would not give Him pain,
They only just passed down the street, and left Him in the rain.

Still Jesus cried, 'Forgive them, for they know not what they do,'
And still it rained the wintry rain that drenched Him through and through;
The crowds went home and left the streets without a soul to see,
And Jesus crouched against a wall and cried for Calvary.

G. A. Studdert Kennedy, *Rhymes* (London:
Hodder & Stoughton, 1929), p. 43.

26 Steve Bruce, *Religion in the Modern World* (Oxford: OUP, 1996), p. 4.
27 For a history and analysis of movements of population within Europe, see
Leslie Page Moch, *Moving Europeans: Migrations in Western Europe since 1650*
(Bloomington, IN: University of Indiana Press, 2003).
28 Alan Billings, *God and Community Cohesion: Help or Hindrance?* (London: SPCK,
2009), chapter 5.
29 As noted by Terry Eagleton, *Reason, Faith and Revolution: Reflections on the
God Debate* (New Haven, CT and London: Yale University Press, 2009), p. 148.
30 Cited in the *Sunday Telegraph*, 18 January 2009.
31 There were many such stories. An article in the *Sunday Telegraph* by Olga
Craig and Patrick Sawer summed them up under the headline, 'Losing our
religion'. *Sunday Telegraph*, 15 February 2009.
32 Poll commissioned by the *Sunday Telegraph*, 31 May 2009.
33 John Micklethwait and Adrian Wooldridge, *God is Back: How the Global Rise
of Faith is Changing the World* (London: Allen Lane, 2009); Eagleton, *Reason,
Faith and Revolution*.
34 Billings, *God and Community Cohesion*, chapter 2.
35 Said by Blair in a BBC television documentary, *The Blair Years*, after
leaving office in 2008.
36 George Herbert, *The Country Parson/The Temple*, ed. and intr. John N. Wall
(New York: Paulist Press, 1981).
37 This is documented in Anthony Russell, *The Clerical Profession* (London:
SPCK, 1980).
38 See Peter L. Berger, 'Secularization and De-secularization', in Linda Woodhead
(ed.), *Religions in the Modern World* (London: Routledge, 2002), pp. 291–8.
39 Bruce, *Religion and Modernization*, p. 6.

2 How the Church thinks about itself

1 The words are those of Robert Bellarmine, a sixteenth-century Jesuit. Quoted
in Avery Dulles, *Models of the Church* (New York: Image, 1978), p. 20.
2 The words are by Frederick William Faber (1814–63), an Anglican priest
and disciple of John Henry Newman who also converted to Roman

Catholicism. There is a Protestant version of the hymn that takes out the Marian references and the Roman Catholic triumphalism.

3 The United Reformed Church has since taken in the Churches of Christ (1981) and the Congregational Union of Scotland (2000) – making about 1,600 local churches with 75,000 members.

4 Richard Hooker, *Of the Laws of Ecclesiastical Polity*, 2 vols (London: Everyman's Library, 1968).

5 For the census data see Owen Chadwick, *The Victorian Church, Part One: 1829–59* (London: SCM Press, 1971), pp. 363–9.

6 See Margaret Harris, *Organizing God's Work: Challenges for Churches and Synagogues* (London: Macmillan, 1999). Professor Harris argues that religious bodies are like any other voluntary organization in secularized societies. People will join them if they meet their needs and leave them if they do not.

7 *Ut Unum Sint*, Papal Encyclical of John Paul II, 25 May 1995, Section 86. Section 97 reads:

> The Catholic Church, both in her *praxis* and in her solemn documents, holds that the communion of the particular Churches with the Church of Rome, and of their Bishops with the Bishop of Rome, is – in God's plan – an essential requisite of full and visible communion. Indeed full communion, of which the Eucharist is the highest sacramental mani-festation, needs to be visibly expressed in a ministry in which all the Bishops recognize that they are united in Christ and all the faithful find confirmation for their faith. The first part of the Acts of the Apostles presents Peter as the one who speaks in the name of the apostolic group and who serves the unity of the community – all the while respecting the authority of James, the head of the Church in Jerusalem. This func-tion of Peter must continue in the Church so that under her sole Head, who is Jesus Christ, she may be visibly present in the world as the communion of all his disciples.

8 Catholic Bishops' Conference of England and Wales, Ireland and Scotland, *One Bread One Body: A Teaching Document on the Eucharist in the Life of the Church, and the Establishment of General Norms on Sacramental Sharing* (Catholic Truth Society and Veritas, 1989).

9 George A. Lindbeck, *The Future of Roman Catholic Theology* (Philadelphia: Fortress; London: SPCK, 1969), p. 27.

10 Henri de Lubac, cited in Christine Hall and Robert Hannaford (eds), *Order and Ministry* (Leominster: Gracewing, 1996), p. 48.

11 The modern church council dates from the Parochial Church Councils Measure 1921, which stated that 'it shall be the duty of the councils in every parish to co-operate with the incumbents in the administration, conduct and development of church work, both within the church and outside'.

12 This is very clear from a reading of 1 Corinthians 12.27.

13 Revelation 1.6; 5.10.

14 1 Peter 2.9.

15 The term is associated with the work of the Roman Catholic scholar Karl Rahner.

16 Kate Zebiri, *British Muslim Converts: Choosing Alternative Lives* (Oxford: Oneworld, 2008), p. 248.

17 This is the thesis of Paul Heelas and Linda Woodhead, *The Spiritual Revolution: Why Religion is Giving Way to Spirituality* (Oxford: Blackwell, 2004).

18 Wade Clark Roof, *Spiritual Marketplace* (Princeton: Princeton University Press, 1999), p. 137. Quoted in Charles Taylor, *A Secular Age* (Cambridge MA and London: Belknap, 2007), p. 508.

19 Heelas and Woodhead list those groups that were meeting in and around Kendal, Cumbria, in 2000–2 in Heelas and Woodhead, *The Spiritual Revolution*, Appendix 3, pp. 156–7.

20 Psalm 34.8.

21 <www.htb.org.uk>.

22 Cited in Hans-Peter Grosshans, *Luther* (London: Fount, 1997), p. 78.

23 1 Corinthians 12.7.

24 The Roman Catholic Church speaks of the lay apostolate.

25 During the course of the last century, new ways of being an ordained minister were developed. Clergy might be full-time and paid – stipendiary – or part-time and unpaid – non-stipendiary, including local ordained ministers and ministers who had a house for duty. The biggest single change, however, was the decision to ordain women. The full implication of this cannot be known, however, until women are able to function at every level, including the episcopate. In addition there have always been clergy who have not exercised a parochial role. I would want to argue that the further an ordained person is from ministry in and with a congregation, the less likely it is that he or she functions as a priest.

3 Classical: the parson

1 Justin Lewis-Anthony, *If You Meet George Herbert on the Road, Kill Him: Radically Re-thinking Priestly Ministry* (London: Mowbray, 2009). The author asserts (p. 1) that 'for 350 years the Church of England has been haunted by a pattern of parochial ministry which is based upon fantasy and has been untenable for more than 100 of those years'. It does seem curious that the Church could have been so fundamentally misguided for so long and not noticed.

2 From 'The Author to the Reader' in George Herbert, *The Country Parson/ The Temple*, ed. and intr. John N. Wall (New York: Paulist Press, 1981), p. 54.

3 Herbert was a parish priest for less than three years (1630–3). His ministry was recalled (idealized and mythologized) by Izaak Walton in his *The Life of Mr George Herbert*, written in 1670.

4 I suspect that what people observe in clergy they admire is still the biggest influence on ordinands and younger clergy, and would take a lot to overcome or modify significantly.

5 The Book of Common Prayer ('Prayer Book') was largely the creation of Archbishop Thomas Cranmer in 1549. It went through several revisions before being reissued in 1662 – the version that remains in use. It was unique in containing all the services of the Church of England in a single volume.

6 Novels such as: Henry Fielding, *Joseph Andrews* (1742); Jane Austen, *Pride and Prejudice* (1813); Anthony Trollope, *Barchester Towers* (1857); George Orwell, *A Clergyman's Daughter* (1935).

7 The Porvoo communion of churches, mostly in Northern Europe, have signed an agreement to 'share a common life in mission and service': the Evangelical-Lutheran Churches of Estonia, Lithuania, Sweden, Norway, Iceland and Finland and the Anglican Churches of Wales, Ireland, Scotland and England. Two churches from Southern Europe also belong: the Lusitanian Church in Portugal and the Reformed Episcopal Church of Spain. The Evangelical Lutheran Churches of Denmark and Latvia have observer status.

8 Article VI, 'Of the Sufficiency of the Holy Scriptures for salvation', from the Thirty-Nine Articles (1662). Emphasis added. The Thirty-Nine Articles were first issued in 1563 as an attempt to define Anglicanism over against Roman Catholicism on the one hand, and Calvinism on the other.

9 Herbert, 'A Prayer after Sermon', *The Country Parson/The Temple*, p. 115.

10 Herbert, *The Country Parson/The Temple*, p. 62.

11 Herbert, *The Country Parson/The Temple*, p. 64.

12 The quotation is from John Milton's poem, 'On the new forces of conscience under the long parliament' (1646):

> Because you have thrown off your Prelate Lord,
> And with stiff vows renounced his liturgy
> To seize the widowed whore Plurality
> From them whose sin ye envied, not abhorred,
> Dare ye for this adjure the civil sword
> To force our consciences that Christ set free,
> And ride us with a classic hierarchy
> Taught ye by mere A. S. and Rutherford?
> Men whose life, learning, faith and pure intent
> Would have been held in high esteem with Paul
> Must now be named and printed heretics
> By shallow Edwards and Scotch what d'ye call:
> But we do hope to find out all your tricks,
> Your plots and packing worse than those of Trent,
> That so the Parliament
> May with their wholesome and preventive shears
> Clip your phylacteries, though balk your ears,
> And succor our just fears
> When they shall read this clearly in your charge:
> New *presbyter* is but old *priest* writ large.

13 Catechism, in *The First English Prayer Book* (New Alresford: Arthur James, 1999), p. 95; A Catechism, Book of Common Prayer (1662).

14 Richard Hooker, *Of the Laws of Ecclesiastical Polity*, 2 vols (London: Everyman's Library, 1968).

15 The Ordering of Priests, Book of Common Prayer (1662).

16 Herbert, *The Country Parson/The Temple*, p. 75.

17 Cited in Anthony Russell, *The Country Parson* (London: SPCK, 1993), p. 64.

18 See Wesley Carr, *The Priestlike Task* (London: SPCK, 1985); *The Pastor as Theologian* (London: SPCK, 1990); *Say One For Me: The Church of England in the Next Decade* (London: SPCK, 1992).

19 Anthony Russell, *The Clerical Profession* (London: SPCK, 1984).

20 Herbert, *The Country Parson/The Temple*, p. 73.

21 Russell, *The Country Parson*, p. 200.

22 The first college was St Bees in Cumbria in 1816.

23 Herbert, *The Country Parson/The Temple*, p. 56.

24 *Faith in the City: Report of the Archbishop's Commission on Urban Priority Areas* (London: Church House, 1985).

25 The younger Tractarians (Keble, Newman, Froude) were, in the main, all for disestablishment, fearing that state control had corrupted the Church. Keble wanted to tell the government, 'Take every pound, shilling and penny, and the curse of sacrilege along with it; only let us make our own bishops, and be governed by our own laws.' Keble to Newman, 8 August 1833. Cited in Owen Chadwick, *The Victorian Church, Part One: 1829–59* (London: SCM, 1971), p. 72.

26 See Christie Davies, 'Moralization and Demoralization: A Moral Explanation for Changes in Crime, Disorder and Social Problems', in Digby Anderson (ed.), *The Loss of Virtue* (London: Social Affairs Unit, 1992), p. 10.

27 The errors included the refusal by modern science and philosophy to submit to supervision by the Church. The Syllabus ends with the Pope declaring his implacable hostility towards 'progress, liberalism and modern civilization'.

28 Horton Davies, *Worship and Theology in England: The Ecumenical Century 1900 to the Present* (Grand Rapids: Eerdmans, 1996).

29 'Blessed Lord, who hast caused all holy Scriptures to be written for our learning; Grant that we may in such wise hear them read, mark, learn, and inwardly digest them, that by patience, and comfort of thy holy Word, we may embrace, and ever hold fast the blessed hope of everlasting life.' The Collect for the Second Sunday in Advent, Book of Common Prayer (1662).

30 Alan Billings, *Secular Lives, Sacred Hearts: The Role of the Church in a Time of No Religion* (London: SPCK, 2004).

4 Evangelical: the minister

1 The Revd Alan Gadd, reported in the *Church Times*, 3 January 1997.

2 For an account and evaluation from a sociological standpoint, see David Martin, *Forbidden Revolutions: Pentecostalism in Latin America, Catholicism in Eastern Europe* (London: SPCK, 1996).

3 D. W. Bebbington, *Evangelicalism in Modern Britain: A History from the 1730s to the 1980s* (London: Routledge, 1993), p. 1.

4 Diarmaid MacCulloch, *Thomas Cranmer* (New Haven, CT and London: Yale University Press, 1996), p. 2.

5 Andrew Brown-Lawson, *John Wesley and the Anglican Evangelicals of the Eighteenth Century: A Study in Co-operation and Separation with Special Reference to the Calvinistic Controversies* (Edinburgh: Pentland Press, 1984).

6 The view I take is that put forward by Bebbington, *Evangelicalism in Modern Britain*.

7 The theology evangelicals reacted against was that which lay behind William Paley's famous teleological argument in defence of theism, in which he used the analogy of the watchmaker. Who, on coming across a watch, would doubt the existence of the watchmaker? By analogy, who, seeing the intricacies of the structure of the universe, would doubt the existence of God? But the watchmaker is not intimately involved in the ongoing actions of the watch. So the analogy suggested a rather remote and uninvolved God.

8 The words are from the hymn, 'Praise the Lord ye heavens adore him' by Thomas Coram (*c.* 1668–1751), a philanthropist who founded the London Foundling Hospital for abandoned children.

9 A point made by Gavin White, *How the Churches Got to Be the Way They Are* (London: SCM, 1990), p. 7.

10 Quoted in Bamber Gascoigne, *The Christians* (London: Jonathan Cape, 1977), pp. 222–3.

11 Cited by Bebbington, *Evangelicalism in Modern Britain*, p. 52.

12 They are described as such in Frances Trollope's novel, *The Vicar of Wrexhill*, 1837, which is designed to discredit the evangelical party.

13 Owen Chadwick, *The Victorian Church, Part One: 1829–59* (London: SCM Press, 1971), p. 441.

14 The evangelical scholar Alister McGrath concurs – see Alister McGrath, *Christian Theology: An Introduction* (Oxford: Blackwell, 1994), p. 111.

15 Cited in G. R. Cragg, *The Church and the Age of Reason (1648–1789)*, The Pelican History of the Church, Vol. 4 (London: Penguin, 1960), p. 142.

16 Chadwick, *The Victorian Church, Part One: 1829–59*, p. 442.

17 From the hymn by Charles Wesley, 'And can it be that I should gain/an interest in the Saviour's blood'.

18 Chadwick, *The Victorian Church, Part One: 1829–59*, p. 443.

19 The phrase is used in two of the Tracts for the Times.

20 This was the position taken by an influential Broad Church publication of 1860, *Essays and Reviews*.

21 Cited in 'The Confessional nature of the Church; 198th General Assembly of the US Presbyterian Church' (1986), in Donald K. McKim (ed.), *Major Themes in the Reformed Tradition* (Grand Rapids: Eerdmans, 1992), p. 23.

22 The hymn is by John Bowring (1792–1872).

23 Graham Kendrick (b. 1950), 'From heaven You came', Copyright © 1983 Thankyou Music. <tym@kingsway.co.uk>. Used by permission.

24 From the hymn 'Rock of ages' by Augustus Toplady (1740–78).

25 T. F. Torrance, *Royal Priesthood: A Theology of Ordained Ministry* (Edinburgh: T&T Clark, 1993), p. 31.

26 Article XIX, 'Of the Church', from the Thirty-Nine Articles (1662).

27 The Ordering of Priests, Book of Common Prayer.

28 Article XXV, 'Of the Sacraments', from the Thirty-Nine Articles (1662).

29 Bebbington, *Evangelicalism in Modern Britain*, p. 229.

30 George Carey, *The Church in the Market Place* (Eastbourne: Kingsway, 1995), p. 15.

31 Testimonials have always formed an important part of evangelical witness.

32 The bishop at the time was David Lunn, though the principal advocate for NOS in the Bishop's Council was Archdeacon Stephen Lowe, who went on to become Bishop of Hulme.

33 Matthew Fox was forbidden to teach by Cardinal Ratzinger (Pope Benedict XVI) in 1988 and expelled from the order in 1992. He has since become an Anglican. Matthew Fox's theology and spirituality is set out in: Matthew Fox, *Original Blessing: Primer in Creation Spirituality* (San Francisco: Bear & Co., 1987). See also <http://www.originallyblessed.org> and <http://www.matthewfox.org>. For a brief history of the Nine O'Clock Service, see Roland Howard, *The Rise and Fall of the Nine O'Clock Service: A Cult within the Church?* (London: Mowbray, 1996).

34 One of the influential societies for conservative evangelicals is Reform: <http://www.reform.org.uk/>.

35 1 John 4.1–6.

36 Matthew 20.25–28.

5 Catholic: the priest

1 E. A. Down, 'The Tractarian Tradition', in N. P. Williams and Charles Harris (eds), *Northern Catholicism: Centenary Studies in the Oxford and Parallel Movements* (London: SPCK, 1933), p. 276.

2 *Report of the First Anglo-Catholic Priests' Convention* (London: The Society of SS Peter and Paul, 1921), p. 177.

3 W. J. Sparrow Simpson, 'The Revival from 1845–1933', in Williams and Harris, *Northern Catholicism*, p. 73.

4 Cited in Robin Greenwood, *Transforming Priesthood: A New Theology of Mission and Ministry* (London: SPCK, 1994), p. 12.

5 Owen Chadwick, *The Mind of the Oxford Movement* (London: A & C Black, 1960), p. 143.

6 The Bull of Leo XIII, *Apostolicae Curae*.

7 29 March 1897.

8 Down, 'The Tractarian Tradition', p. 277.

9 John 10.3.

10 Chadwick, *The Mind of the Oxford Movement*, p. 197.

11 Chadwick, *The Mind of the Oxford Movement*, p. 197.

12 Articles XXVIII and XXXI.

13 Donald Gray, *Earth and Altar: The Evolution of the Parish Communion in the Church of England to 1945* (Norwich: Canterbury Press, for Alcuin Club, 1986), p. 199.

14 A. G. Hebert, *Liturgy and Society: The Function of the Church in the Modern World* (London: Faber & Faber, 1935), and A. G. Hebert (ed.), *The Parish Communion: A Book of Essays* (London: SPCK, 1937).

15 Adrian Hastings, *A History of English Christianity 1920–1970* (London: SCM, 1991), p. 33.

16 The Ordering of Priests, Book of Common Prayer.
17 Incarnational thinking inspired the work of catholic Anglican theologians such as Charles Gore and Michael Ramsey. It was also influential in the theology of William Temple, Leslie Houlden and Stephen Sykes.
18 H. Maynard Smith, *Frank Bishop of Zanzibar: Life of Frank Weston DD, 1871–1924* (London: SPCK, 1926), p. 302.
19 *Church Times*, August 1922.
20 Joseph Williamson, *Father Joe* (London: Hodder & Stoughton, 1963), p. 120.
21 Quoted in Francis Penhale, *Catholics in Crisis* (London: Mowbray, 1986), p. 69.
22 Penhale, *Catholics in Crisis*, p. 74.
23 For a contemporary evaluation of the biblical material, see Kevin Giles, *What on Earth is the Church? A Biblical and Theological Inquiry* (London: SPCK, 1995).
24 Francis Underhill, in Williams and Harris, *Northern Catholicism*, p. 290.
25 E. L. Mascall, *Women Priests?* (London: Church Literature Association, 1972), p. 24.
26 The answers to these questions proved to be 'Yes' and 'On the whole'. Damage was done to Anglican–Roman Catholic relations and it is hard to see how the Anglican Church can go on thinking of itself as a 'bridge' church when it has put itself at such odds with both the Roman Catholic and Orthodox Churches on this issue. Most Anglicans, however, including catholic Anglicans, seem to have taken women's ordination in their stride.
27 Cited in John Shelton Reed, *Glorious Battle: The Cultural Politics of Victorian Anglo-Catholicism* (Nashville, TN and London: Vanderbilt University Press, 1996), p. 128.
28 Reed, *Glorious Battle*, pp. 22–3.
29 Reed, *Glorious Battle*, p. 141.
30 Martyn Percy, *Clergy: The Origin of Species* (London: Continuum, 2006), p. 146.

6 Utility: the social activist and personal therapist

1 Charles Gore (ed.), *Lux Mundi: A Series of Studies in the Religion of the Incarnation*, 3rd edn (London: John Murray, 1890).
2 Reinhold Niebuhr identified the problem in part in *Moral Man and Immoral Society: A Study in Ethics and Politics* (London and New York: Charles Scribner's Sons, 1934).
3 The Archbishop of Canterbury's Commission on Urban Priority Areas, *Faith in the City: A Call for Action by Church and Nation* (London: Church House, 1985).
4 From the Declaration in the Ordering of Priests, The Alternative Service Book 1980.
5 In the eighteenth century it was the duty of the churchwardens to bring to church courts those guilty of adultery, fornication or incest. Public penance was required. Parson Woodforde records in his diary for 3 February 1768: 'Sarah Gore came to me this morning and brought me an instrument from the Court at Wells to perform publick penance next Sunday at Castle

Cary church for having a child.' Public penance was to be dressed in a white sheet, holding a taper and confessing guilt. For a full account of the various law-enforcement roles of the clergy, see Anthony Russell, *The Clerical Profession* (London: SPCK, 1980).

6 Peter Green, *The Town Parson* (London: Longmans, Green & Co., 1919), pp. 34–5.

7 George Herbert, *The Country Parson/The Temple*, ed. and intr. John N. Wall (New York: Paulist Press, 1981), chapter entitled 'The Parson in Circuit'.

8 Green, *The Town Parson*, p. 25.

9 All denominations experienced decline, though it was some time before the Roman Catholic Church in Britain realized that it was in the same position as other churches. For a while, Roman Catholics seemed more successful in holding their existing membership, while inward migration boosted overall numbers.

10 For an account of the New Age Movement, see Paul Heelas, *The New Age Movement* (Oxford: Blackwell, 1996). For a sociologist's account of religion in contemporary Britain, see Grace Davie, *Religion in Britain since 1945: Believing without Belonging* (Oxford: Blackwell, 1994); Steve Bruce, *Religion in Modern Britain* (Oxford: OUP, 1995).

11 See Alan Billings, 'Keeping Chaos at Bay: The Place of Ritual and Community in the Events of Hillsborough', *Crucible* (Board for Social Responsibility January–March 1990), pp. 4ff.

12 I use 'social activist' to mean those who engage in politics and social issues at a level wider than the local community. I use 'community activist' to mean those who have a more geographically local community focus, rather than a wider issues focus – though most community activists probably are social activists as well!

13 This is the thrust of Harvey Cox, *The Secular City: Secularization and Urbanization in Theological Perspective* (London: SCM, 1965).

14 Dietrich Bonhoeffer, *Letters and Papers from Prison* (London: Fontana, 1962); Paul van Buren, *The Secular Meaning of the Gospel* (London: SCM, 1963); John Robinson, *Honest to God* (London: SCM, 1963).

15 Amos 5.24.

16 Liberation Theology was introduced to English readers with the publication of Gustavo Gutiérrez, *A Theology of Liberation: History, Politics, and Salvation* (New York: Orbis, 1973). An English evangelical version of the same theme is David Sheppard, *Bias to the Poor* (London: Hodder & Stoughton, 1983).

17 Archbishop of Canterbury's Commission, *Faith in the City*.

18 Noel Malcolm, 'The inherent justice of taking occasional pot-shots at the clergy', *The Spectator*, 14 May 1988.

19 For community work in a rural setting, see John Reader, *Local Theology: Church and Community in Dialogue* (London: SPCK, 1994). For a critique of the whole approach from the point of view of right-wing critics, see Digby Anderson, *The Kindness that Kills: The Churches' Simplistic Response to Complex Social Issues* (London: SPCK, 1984).

20 A succinct introduction to Liberation Theology, its origins and methods, can be found in Stephen Pattison, *Pastoral Care and Liberation Theology* (Cambridge: CUP, 1994), part 1. For an account of British Liberation Theology, see Chris Rowland and John Vincent, *Liberation Theology UK* (Sheffield: Urban Theology Unit, 1995). For an example of the method in practice, see Laurie Green, *Power to the Powerless: Theology Brought to Life* (Basingstoke: Marshall Pickering, 1987).

21 For a critique of the whole approach see H. M. Kuitert, *Everything is Politics but Politics is not Everything: A Theological Perspective on Faith and Politics* (London: SCM, 1986).

22 There is a scholarly debate as to whether changed behaviour is the result of religion or people who are intent on self-improvement are drawn towards religion as support. See Rodney Stark, *The Victory of Reason: How Christianity Led to Freedom, Capitalism, and Western Success* (New York: Random House, 2005), pp. 230–1; Arthur F. McGovern, *Liberation Theology and Its Critics: Toward an Assessment* (Maryknoll, NY: Orbis, 1989).

23 The quotations are from Laurie Green, *Let's Do Theology* (London: Mowbray, 1990). Green, *Power to the Powerless*, is a revealing account of how a Birmingham congregation was politicized by their parish priest.

24 Pierre-Joseph Proudhon (1809–65), an important early self-designated anarchist, said that 'Property is theft' in his book, *What is Property? An Inquiry into the Principle of Right and of Government*, trans. by B. R. Tucker (Princeton, MA: B. R. Tucker, 1876; first published in French in 1840 as *Qu'est-ce que la propriété?*).

25 For a full discussion of these and other points by a philosopher, see Gordon Graham, *The Idea of Christian Charity: A Critique of some Contemporary Conceptions* (London: Collins, 1990), chapter 3.

26 These trends are well brought out in Christopher Lasch, *The Culture of Narcissism: American Life in an Age of Diminishing Expectations* (New York: Norton, 1979); and Frank Furedi, *Therapy Culture: Cultivating Vulnerability in an Anxious Age* (London: Routledge, 2004).

27 Alastair Campbell, *Rediscovering Pastoral Care* (London: Darton, Longman & Todd, 1981).

28 Howard Clinebell, *Growth Counselling* (Nashville, TN: Abingdon Press, 1979), p. 17. See also H. Clinebell, *Self-understanding through Psychology and Religion* (New York: Abingdon Press, 1951) and *Basic Types of Pastoral Counselling: New Resources for Ministering to the Troubled* (Nashville, TN: Abingdon Press, 1966). Critics of an over-reliance on psychology in pastoral care include Thomas C. Oden, *Care of Souls in the Classic Tradition* (Philadelphia: Fortress, 1984) and R. A. Lambourne, 'An Objection to the Proposed National Pastoral Organisation', in Michael Wilson (ed.), *Explorations in Health and Salvation: A Selection of Papers by Bob Lambourne* (Birmingham: University of Birmingham, Institute for the Study of Worship and Religious Architecture, 1983).

29 Campbell, *Rediscovering Pastoral Care*, p. 10.

30 Campbell, *Rediscovering Pastoral Care*, p. 15.

31 Campbell, *Rediscovering Pastoral Care*, p. 15.

32 Jeffrey Masson, *Against Therapy* (London: Fontana, 1988), p. 299.

33 Campbell, *Rediscovering Pastoral Care*, p. 16.

34 Wesley Carr, *Say One for Me: The Church of England in the Next Decade* (London: SPCK, 1992), p. 16.

7 Making God possible in the twenty-first century

1 The profile is by Daniel Zalewski, an editor of the *New Yorker*. Quoted in *The Guardian*, 16 February 2009.

2 Fundamentalism is a word that has now been stretched to encompass those who hold certain types of belief across all religions. It originated among conservative Christians, chiefly in the USA at the end of the nineteenth century, who reacted to biblical and historical criticism by calling for a return to the 'fundamentals'. These included the idea that the Bible was incapable of error. For a definition and discussion of fundamentalism in its stretched sense, see Peter Herriot, *Religious Fundamentalism: Global, Local and Personal* (London: Routledge, 2009), pp. 4–5.

3 The Society of Jesus and the Governors of Preston Catholic College were taken to court in 2009 by a City solicitor and former pupil, Patrick Raggett. He alleged that he was sexually abused by a priest at the college in the 1960s, and was given leave to sue even though the incidents happened over 30 years ago. Other cases are likely to follow. In the Irish Republic in 2009, the Child Abuse Commission, set up in 2000, finally reported into widespread abuse, physical and sexual, of children in various institutions under the control of religious orders. The report documented abuses that had been going on since the 1930s in industrial schools, homes for the disabled and day schools. The abuse was systemic. Both Church and state turned a blind eye. See also Colm O'Gorman, *Beyond Belief* (London: Hodder & Stoughton, 2009).

4 Evidence from the Burnley Project shows a contrast between the attitudes towards religion of Asian Muslim young people and white 'Christian' young people in selected northern towns. The Asian youngsters were generally interested in all faiths and thought religion important. The white young people were largely indifferent towards religion and some were hostile towards non-Christian faiths. Alan Billings, *God and Community Cohesion. Help or Hindrance?* (London: SPCK, 2009), pp. 56–61.; Andrew Holden, *Religious Cohesion in Times of Conflict: Christian–Muslim Relations in Segregated Towns* (London: Continuum, 2009), pp. 26–58.

5 Steve Bruce, *God is Dead: Secularization in the West* (Oxford: Blackwell, 2002), p. 193.

6 The point is made by Michael J. Buckley, SJ, *At the Origins of Modern Atheism* (New Haven, CT and London: Yale University Press, 1987).

7 Justin Martyr, *c.* 100–65 CE, *First Apology*.

8 I had several conversations with him on the matter in the years just prior to his death in 2008.

9 John Gray, *Straw Dogs: Thoughts on Humans and Other Animals* (London: Granta, 2002), p. xi.

10 British Humanist Association, *The Meaning of Life, and 'For the one life we have'* (BHA, 1 Gower Street, London WC1E 6HD).

11 See, for example, Matthew 23.13, 14, 15, 23, 25, 27, 29, with its repeated, 'Woe to you, scribes and Pharisees, hypocrites!'.

12 Terry Eagleton, *Reason, Faith and Revolution: Reflections on the God Debate* (New Haven, CT and London: Yale University Press, 2009), p. 16.

13 Roger Trigg, *Ideas of Human Nature: An Historical Introduction* (Oxford: Blackwell, 1988).

14 For the theory of Gaia, see James Lovelock, *Gaia: The Practical Science of Planetary Medicine* (London: Gaia Books, 1991).

15 This is the charge of Gray, *Straw Dogs*.

16 Peter Singer, *Re-thinking Life and Death: The Collapse of our Traditional Ethics* (Oxford: OUP, 1994).

17 Alan Billings, *Secular Lives, Sacred Hearts: The Role of the Church in a Time of No Religion* (London: SPCK, 2004).

18 Matthew Parris, 'A funeral teaches me that Gray was wrong in his elegy about the loneliness of virtue', *The Spectator*, 9 May 2009.

19 Melanie Reid, 'Hospitals never needed God more', *The Times*, 7 April 2009.

20 Charles Taylor, *A Secular Age* (Cambridge, MA and London: Belknap, 1997), p. 423.

21 The first amendment to the American constitution, 1791.

22 All presidential speeches are available on the White House website: <http://www.whitehouse.gov>.

23 <http://www.whitehouse.gov>.

24 This is the conclusion of Stephen Mansfield, *The Faith of Barack Obama* (Nashville, TN: Thomas Nelson, 2008), chapter 4.

25 <http://www.whitehouse.gov>.

26 Psalm 121.1, AV.

27 Deuteronomy 34.

28 The principle was re-affirmed in 2004 when the wearing of 'conspicuous religious symbols' in state schools was banned. This included the wearing of distinctive religious dress – such as the hijab and jilbab – by Muslim girls.

29 Since 1976 doctrine and liturgy have been the sole responsibility of Synod.

30 The church has taken up a number of causes in post-war Britain, such as the plight of the urban priority areas (*Faith in the City*) and third-world debt.

31 The Professor of Divinity at Edinburgh University has said that establishment is no longer tenable. David Fergusson, *Church and State and Civil Society* (Cambridge: CUP, 2004), pp. 186ff.

32 Milan Kundera, *The Book of Laughter and Forgetting* (London: Faber & Faber, 1996), p. 235.

33 Timothy Jenkins, in a paper given to the Cambridge Theological Society in 2007, cited in Ben Quash, 'The Anglican Church as a Polity of Presence', in Duncan Dormer, Jack McDonald and Jeremy Caddick (eds), *Anglicanism: The Answer to Modernity* (London and New York: Continuum, 2003), pp. 46–7.

Index

Index